MW00984209

This is a painting that Ray Mears commissioned artist Phil Lavely of UT-Martin to paint. Mears dedicated it to his three sons—Steve, Michael and Matthew.

RAY MEARS'

BIG ORANGE MEMORIES

How Ray Mears Transformed
Tennessee Sports Traditions

Ron Bliss

OFFICIALLY APPROVED
BY THE MEARS FAMILY

TENNESSEE VALLEY
Publishing®
2007

Copyright © 2007 Ron Bliss

All rights reserved. No part of this book may be reproduced in any form or by any electronic or mechanical means including information storage and retrieval systems without permission in writing from the author except by a reviewer who may quote brief passages in a review.

Published by:

Tennessee Valley Publishing
P.O. Box 52527
Knoxville, Tennessee 37950-2527
www.TVP1.com

Printed and bound in the United States of America.

Library of Congress Control Number: 2007934419

ISBN - 13: 978-1-932604-50-4
ISBN - 10: 1-932604-50-2

Cover design by Barry T. Armstrong.

Dedication

This book is dedicated to Robert M. Mears, my father, who gave up his boyhood for his immediate family. When he was in the seventh grade, his father, a steel-mill worker, lost a leg in a trolley car accident. To stay off welfare, my dad took his dad's place in the steel mill. He lost his youth to the mill and never played any sports. He never had the experience of attending junior high or high school.

He taught me to be thrifty because he would never give me a dime for a movie. To have enough money, I had to start working early and develop good work habits. The greatest of all my strengths today is my mental toughness, which was one of my dad's greatest strengths as testified by only missing one day of work in 46 years. He was a great perfectionist. When I asked to help around the house by mowing the grass, he said, "Don't touch that mower. Go out and play ball." Our lawn was the neatest on the block because he mowed it up and back and at a diagonal, three different ways. He never played ball with me because he didn't know how. His was a great sacrifice.

I'd also like to dedicate the book to my three sons. Steve is vice president of a bank, Michael is an electrical engineer and Matthew is a veternarian. With my obsession for spending time with my players, they lost out on a close relationship with their dad. Hopefully, they learned good qualities from being near me and watching me coach.

Ramon A. Mears

RAMON A. MEARS

Ray Mears in his "Big Orange Room" at home on Tellico Lake near Knoxville, Tennessee. This photograph was taken in 2000 when text for this book was being developed by Ray Mears and the author.

Stokely Athletic Center

Ray Mears' winning basketball program and flair for promoting his teams through the use of entertaining pre-game shows were instrumental in the expansion of the University of Tennessee's Armory-Fieldhouse to the 12,700 seat Stokely Athletic Center. A $500,000 gift from industrialist William B. Stokely helped fund the $1.5 million expansion which was completed in 1966.

Stokely was the home of many great teams, including several SEC championship teams. It proved to be a great venue for displaying Mears' basketball and marketing wizardry. Mears took Tennessee basketball to heights it had never seen before. One of his crowning achievements was recruiting and developing the basketball skills of Ernie Grunfeld and Bernard King—two All-American players on the same team. The Ernie and Bernie Show broke many school records and made UT, for the first time, a household word in the college basketball world.

Table of Contents

List of Photographs

Foreword

When Ray neared retirement, he thought only of returning to East Tennessee where he once more could attend UT football, UT basketball and other university events. Mike Edwards, former star Vol, introduced Ray to a lake community not far from Knoxville. Ray loved the beauty of the water and mountains and even planned to play golf, so he found his perfect home.

A goal of his retirement years was to write another book, this time recounting the fifteen successful years as basketball coach at the University of Tennessee. He found an enthusiastic writer in Ron Bliss and the two of them spent hours-upon-hours compiling stories and pictures of those wonderful years. The results of their work is contained in this book. Our family hopes you will enjoy reliving *Big Orange Memories*.

Sincerely,

Dana, Steve, Mike and Matt Mears

Introduction

There was the "Wizard of Westwood," and the "Baron of the Bluegrass." John Wooden of UCLA and Adolph Rupp of Kentucky are renowned for their college basketball coaching success.

Tennessee also had its "Barnum of Basketball," who was a contemporary of the other two and could well have joined them in the all-time record books had depression caused by a chemical imbalance not cut short his coaching career at age 51 in 1977. At the time, Ray Mears had a national championship to his credit. He took Wittenberg College of Springfield, Ohio to the NCAA Small College title in 1961 and had a 399-135 career record. This .747 winning percentage still ranks 17th all-time in the NCAA Basketball Record Book.

Mears was third among active coaches, based on winning percentage in the early 1970s. When Rupp retired in 1972 and Wooden in 1975, he served as the nation's winningest active coach the final two years of his career at Tennessee. Dean Smith of North Carolina was challenging him for the spot when he was forced to step down because of his health.

Mears put Tennessee on the basketball map and was the man who encouraged Tennessee fans to start wearing the school's colors when they came to sporting events.

There was little basketball tradition before he arrived in 1962—only one 20-win season in its history and no NCAA trips. The only other success the basketball program enjoyed, until Tennessee qualified for four straight NCAA tournaments under Jerry Green (1998, 1999, 2000 and 2001), was in the early 1980s when Mears' successor, Don DeVoe, produced six more 20-win seasons and six NCAA trips before the well went dry on him.

Tennessee experienced another drought from 2002 until Bruce Pearl arrived for the 2005-2006 season. Pearl has now taken the Vols to back-to-back NCAA tournaments and made the Sweet 16 in 2007.

Coach Pearl is seen by many as a second coming of Mears. Like Mears, he won a small-college national title, before accepting the Wisconsin-Milwaukee job, and emulates Mears' marketing skills. Pearl helped make publication of this book possible by bringing Mears back into the spotlight and wearing the orange jacket that Mears donned in his heyday.

The Mears Years are still considered the glory years of the program. In his tenure, Mears produced a 278-112 record, a winning percentage of .713, and had seven 20-win seasons in an era when only conference champions advanced to the NCAA tournament and only a select few to the then-prestigious NIT. His teams advanced to the NCAA tournament three times, including his final two when Ernie Grunfeld and Bernard King were household words nationally and graced the cover of *Sports Illustrated* as the "Double Trouble From Tennessee."

Mears also produced seven second-place SEC teams in his 15 years at Tennessee, took three teams to the National Invitational Tournament and two others to the National Collegiate Invitational Tournament designed for major-college runners-up in the mid-1970s. Based on records and finishes of his teams and today's standards, 13 of his 15 teams at Tennessee would have almost certainly been invited to the NCAA tournament.

Mears was told early in his career by then *Knoxville News-Sentinel* sports editor Tom Siler that his job was to beat Rupp and Kentucky. He responded, posting a 15-15 record against the Wildcats and beat Rupp seven of the first 11 times their teams met. Included was an upset of Rupp's previously unbeaten "Rupp's Runts" in 1966. Rupp, after his retirement, honored Mears by calling him "The best basketball coach in the nation."

Mears was both successful and colorful. He not only brought victories to the basketball court, but fans to the stands with his marketing approach for the "Big Orange" that was ahead of its time. He made attending basketball games fun for the fans.

Combining the flare for the dramatic that he styled after former Cleveland Indians owner and fellow Ohioan Bill Veeck and his love for the circus, Mears provided a pre-game show that included a 70-piece marching band, baton-twirling majorettes, pom-pom waving Rally Girls and a juggler on a unicycle. He also introduced use of the pep band at college basketball games. He even arranged for a man to wrestle a bear between games of the Vol Classic as a way to draw fans to the stands.

When Mears arrived, the Tennessee basketball team had finished 4-19 the previous season and had drawn just 400 fans to its final regular-season game. With that in mind, Mears felt a flare for the dramatic was in order if he was ever going to kindle the spirit in Tennessee basketball. His actions earned him such nicknames as "Barnum of Basketball" and "Cecil B. DeMears" and his pre-game show the nickname "The Ziegfeld Vol-Lies."

Not only did Mears win and make his basketball games fun for the fans, he produced All-Americans from the young men he recruited. In his 15 years, he produced nine All-

Americans—headed by Ernie Grunfeld and Bernard King, who both went on to enjoy much success in the NBA. Grunfeld also played on the 1976 U.S. Olympic team. Mears did it by using his "Star System," where each player on the team had a role and his scorers enjoyed the glory.

A Mears' contribution that transcended what he did for the basketball program, was his coining of the phrase "Big Orange Country" and his influence that started Vol fans wearing the school's orange and white colors while attending all University of Tennessee games; not just basketball.

This is Ray Mears' story. It's the story of a *legend*.

Photo by Donnell Field

Coach Mears with author, Ron Bliss, *at left*, in 2000.

Acknowledgments

Information for use in this book was drawn from a number of sources, including *The Basketball Vols* by Ben Byrd, *Mears: Portrait of a Tennessee Legend* by Dennis W. Rubright, *It's All In The State of Mind, The Basketball Notebook of Coach Ray Mears, The University of Tennessee Basketball and Football Media Guides, The Wittenberg University Men's Basketball Guide* and the *NCAA Men's Basketball Record Book.*

Thanks goes to the Tennessee Sports Information office, which provided photographs of Mears and the players from his era and Mears' many former players and acquaintances who took their time to give their recollections of Coach Mears to help ensure that his name lives on in college sports history.

Also, thanks to the Ray Mears Family who have so graciously worked with the author to get this effort completed and to Larry V. Roberts for his advice and support.

Donnell Field took pictures at the Mears' home in Loudon that appear in this publication. Also included are University of Tennessee pictures by Elizabeth Olivier of the UTSports.com staff and photographs taken by UT photographers during the Mears' era. A special thanks to Bud Ford, Associate Athletic Director, Media Relations, who graciously provided many of the photographs that are shown in this book. Credit lines are shown for each photograph, except for those provided from the Mears' family collection. All photographs presented in this book not having a specific credit line identified are provided from the Mears' family collection.

Chapter 1

The Man Behind the Traditions

I t was the opening day of the Knoxville Tip-Off Club at Calhoun's On The River in January of 2006. The legendary John Ward, who from 1964 through 1999 was the "Voice of the Vols," was the speaker.

It was a rare occasion for John to come speak to a group. He had kept a low profile for the most part since retiring—going out of his way to stay out of the public eye to allow Bob Kesling, his replacement as the "Voice of the Vols," to make his own name.

But this was something important to Ward. He had seen the glory years of Tennessee basketball and with Bruce Pearl the head coach, he could see a possible return to the heyday enjoyed in the late 1960s and 1970s under another Tennessee basketball coach, **Ray Mears**. To Ward, it was important that the facts on Mears be known.

**John Ward with Coach Ray Mears and Ray's wife Dana
upon Ray's induction into the Tennessee Sports Hall of fame.**

1

Men's basketball had played second fiddle to football in the Tennessee sports family for years, but Ward took the occasion to remind the overflow crowd of more than 400 in attendance (including Pearl, who was just two months into his new job) that the Vols owe a lot of their tradition to basketball and to Ray Mears, in particular.

"People think of this as being a football school, but basketball has played a prominent role in the traditions of the school," noted Ward.

"You go to Tennessee football games on Saturday afternoon and it's a sea of orange. But before Ray Mears arrived in 1962, the only orange you would see at a Tennessee football game would be a letterman wearing his orange sweater," said Ward.

"When Ray Mears came, he looked for a way to get fans interested in basketball. He talked with me and asked me for some ideas. Davy Crockett was big at the time and I suggested we put the players in Coonskin Caps. He said that would never sell. He asked what the mascot was. I told him it was a Volunteer and he told me that would never sell. But the color orange, he said, he could do something with and I told him 'That will never sell.'"

Ward chuckled when he said it. Perhaps it was one of the poorest conclusions he ever reached. Mears decided to go there, despite Ward's words, and the rest is history.

At that time, cigarette advertising was prominent on billboards. It was still several years before cigarette ads were limited in the media and one of the most prominent displays was the Marlboro ad that read: "This is Marlboro Country!"

Mears took that idea and put his own twist on it: "This is Big Orange Country!" It was placed on billboards that people would see as they entered Knoxville.

Mears had come from Ohio, where a high school there used the phrase: "Big Red Country." If Steubenville, Ohio could be "Big Red Country" then Knoxville qualified as "Big Orange Country."

To promote the idea of wearing orange, Mears started the "Orange Tie Club" in 1966. Jim Haslam, who now heads Pilot Oil that is based in Knoxville, was the first president of Mears' Orange Tie Club.

"Now, when you see that sea of orange at a Tennessee football game, you'll know from where it came," said Ward.

Ward noted that famed broadcast friend Keith Jackson said Tennessee's pre-game football tradition has to rank among the best anywhere—the running through the "T" and the band marching to Neyland Stadium. But those, too, came from Mears.

"It was Ray Mears who first had his players run through the 'T' at Stokley Arena," said Ward. "Back at Wittenberg, he had his team run through the 'W' and brought the idea to Knoxville.

"Mears also had the band march into Stokely Arena and would march around the court playing while the opposing team was warming up. That started in 1967 and lasted until the SEC banned it in 1969 after complaints from the other teams. Now, the band marches into Neyland Stadium for football."

Tennessee settled for having a pep band at games after that.

Maybe the thing most associated with Tennessee—the fight song "Rocky Top"—also emerged in the Mears' Era, though Mears couldn't claim it for his own like he could other traditions. But it did gain popularity from a basketball game.

"Tennessee's basketball team finished second in the SEC in 1974 and settled for a tournament called the Conference Coaches' Association in St. Louis, where they played Indiana in the first round," said Ward, noting that only 16 teams made the NCAA tournament in those days.

"The Tennessee pep band went along and played a jazzed up version of the song, along with several others. The fans loved it and asked them to play it again and again. Now it is widely recognized as Tennessee's fight song, but it was first played in its current version at a basketball game."

Roy Harmon of Kingsport, now an executive with Bank of Tennessee, first heard the song the next season at a Tennessee game. He was a student at the time.

"They kept playing it all the time and I remember thinking: 'Why are they playing that? It's not even our fight song,'" said Harmon. "They would play it again and again and again."

One of the reasons given for not printing this book in 2000 was that, supposedly, Mears had been out of the spotlight too long. No one remembered who he was.

But from the day of John Ward's speech, Coach Pearl picked up the gauntlet and made sure Tennessee fans, and others, didn't forget the man who had made "Orange" such a prominent color with Tennessee athletics.

Two weeks later, on February 1, 2006, Pearl broke out an orange jacket to wear in the game against Vanderbilt. Tennessee won, 69-62, in Thompson-Boling Arena.

Pearl said he called the ailing Mears to ask him permission to do it.

"I asked if he'd rather have me wear it just against Kentucky or against Kentucky and Vanderbilt and he said against Kentucky and Vanderbilt," said Pearl in his post-game press conference. The wearing of the jacket at the game was not promoted ahead of time.

"I bring this up because the Vanderbilt program is a very good one and Coach Mears considered them the same as Kentucky," added Pearl.

Coach Bruce Pearl has brought back traditions from the Mears' era.

Chapter 2

Basketball or Bust

Ray Mears, who was born on November 8, 1926, was just five-foot tall and 99 pounds while at Dover High School in Ohio. Those were hardly numbers that attract the interest of major college coaches. But Mears was never one to be told he couldn't do something. He operated on the theory that it wasn't the size of the man in the fight, but the size of the fight in the man that mattered.

Early on, Mears took a liking to an anonymous poem that was also a favorite of late great Alabama football coach Paul "Bear" Bryant:

It's All In The State Of Mind

"If you think you're better, you are.
If you think you dare not, you don't.
If you'd like to win but think you can't
It's almost a 'cinch' you won't.
If you think you'll lose, you've lost.
For out in the world, you'll find success
Begins with a fellow's will – IT'S ALL IN THE
STATE OF MIND.
If you think you're outclassed, you are.
You've got to think high to rise.
You've got to be sure of yourself before
You can ever win the prize.
Life's battles don't always go to the
Stronger or faster man
But sooner or later, the man who wins is
The fellow who thinks he can."

Anonymous

Mears grew up in the steel-mill town of Dover in the east central part of the state south of Canton and northeast of Columbus. His father worked in the steel mill all of his life and that appeared to be Ray's future, unless he could set himself apart and make something of himself in basketball.

Mears' size was a hindrance, but his fire got the attention of his Dover High coach, Dutch Furbay. As fate would have it, Mears tested positive for tuberculosis his sophomore year and wasn't allowed to play basketball on the team. Furbay suggested he coach a team of fifth and sixth graders in the city league. Mears coached one of four teams. The other three were coached by ex-Dover players in their 40s.

"They each had a son on their teams," said Mears. "But, unfortunately, they worked and didn't have time to read about strategy. Fortunately, I did and went on to win the city tournament. This was my first day in the sun as a coach."

It was the first taste of success for the young Mears and whetted his appetite for more coaching in the years to come.

Despite his size, Mears started for Dover at point guard his senior year. After high school, Mears went to work in the steel mill and worked for 16 months to save enough money for college. By now, his goal was clear. He wanted to go to college and learn to become a basketball coach.

Mears grew up and first played basketball at Dover High School in Ohio.

Mears attended Miami of Ohio in Oxford, northwest of Cincinnati. He walked onto the basketball team, feeling he needed to play college ball if he ever hoped to coach it.

Ex-Miami of Ohio All-American Glen Kessler, who was returning as a World War II veteran, took a liking to the young Mears and worked him out daily on outdoor courts in the fall to condition him and prepare him for a tryout on Coach Blue Foster's team. Kessler then talked to Foster and gave him a recommendation that helped him be one of only two players selected from preseason tryouts out of over 100 aspiring athletes.

"Coach Blue Foster formed a group of five players 5'8" and under," said Mears, "and called us *The Firefighters*. We entered the game as a unit and put out the fire."

Ara Parsheghian, who went on to fame as head football coach at Notre Dame, was one of Mears' fellow firefighters.

Mears was named captain of *The Firefighters*, whose job it was to perk up the team if the starters got sluggish. They wreaked havoc on the opposing team for several minutes at a time and gave the five starters a rest.

But all was not hunky-dory. Eight games into his senior season, Mears and Mickey McDade, a scholarship player, were cut from the team by Foster.

"He cut any senior who was not starting," said Mears. "What's amazing is that I don't think something like that ever happened anywhere else. He just called me in one day and said 'I'm going to cut you.' It was earth-shaking to me, but it toughened me."

Mears as a player at Miami of Ohio.

"We had a guy on the team named Bobby Brown, who was the leading scorer in the nation. He offered to go to Coach Foster and try to get me back on the team, but I told him I didn't want back on the team."

So Mears' college career was over, but he'd gotten what he wanted out of it. He could now coach with a playing career as part of his resume.

**Mears *(number 15)* was a member of the 1946-1947
Miami University team that also included Ara Parsheghian *(number 25)*.**

**Mears stayed in contact with former Miami teammate Ara Parsheghian.
Clark Gable was a native of Cadiz, Ohio where Mears got his first coaching job.**

After graduating from Miami in 1949, Mears got his first paid coaching job at Cadiz High School, a short distance from his hometown of Dover and hometown of actor Clark Gable. Mears' tenure lasted just one year. In October of 1950, he was summoned to two years of military duty. His Cadiz team finished 7-14, but it was a start for the twenty-four-year-old Mears who also served as offensive coordinator on the Cadiz football squad which posted a 6-0 record before Mears left for military duty.

Mears with his first team at Cadiz High School in Cadiz, Ohio.

Mears later confided that he thought he could have been a successful football coach, had he chosen to coach that sport. One of his heroes in football coaching was Woody Hayes, who later became a Hall of Fame coach at Ohio State.

When Mears was discharged from the U.S. Army in 1952, he applied for the vacant basketball post at West Tech High in Cleveland. Miami track coach Jim Gordon had ties at West Tech and helped Ray get the job though he had only one year of coaching experience. Mears stayed in Cleveland for four years and revived a program that had experienced little success. His first squad started out 13-1 before settling for second place behind St. Ignatius, whose only regular-season loss came against Mears' team.

Mears' best season came three years later when his team, though made up mostly of underclassmen, made it to the regional by upsetting 18-2 Lorain. Don Wolfe's 26 points and 24 from Frank Davis led West Tech to a 77-69 upset and a berth in Ohio's Sweet 16. The Cinderella ride (his team entered the playoffs at 9-12) ended in the Sweet 16 when unbeaten cross-town rival East Tech ended West Tech's run.

It's interesting to note East Tech that year made it to the Final Four where it lost to Middletown—a team led by a guy named Jerry Lucas. Lucas scored 53 points in the win over East Tech.

Lucas, of course, went on to glory with Ohio State where one of his teammates was the man who succeeded Mears at Tennessee—Don DeVoe.

Lucas also played for years in the NBA.

The Hayes were fellow Ohioans and friends of Coach Mears.

Chapter 3

The Wittenberg Wonder

Mears had gotten the job at West Tech, though he'd coached just one season of high school ball previously. But the twenty-nine-year-old Mears used it as a stepping-stone to his first collegiate job at Wittenberg College. Mears was given a $5,000 salary—a lot of money in those days—to not only coach the basketball team, but serve as ends coach in football and as Wittenberg's tennis director.

Ironically, Mears was not the first choice for the job.

"They gave the job to Frank Shannon, who had been a player at Wittenberg (1938-1940)," said Mears, "But they gave him a car to remain at the high school where he was coaching, so he turned down the Wittenberg job. That was a big thing back in those days. The car was probably equal in value to what he made an entire year coaching."

Mears said it was another twist of fate in his journey toward the top of the college coaching ranks.

"That one was spookier than any of the others," said Mears.

But with yet another door opening, Mears was quick to take advantage.

Mears shot for the moon from the beginning. Upon his arrival, he announced at an alumni meeting that his goal was to win a national championship. Few took him seriously in light of the fact the Tigers had lost 26 of their previous 39 games and had only three winning seasons in the previous nine.

What Mears did at Wittenberg was a precursor of what Tennessee fans could expect in the future. Borrowing a page from Bill Veeck's history for showmanship, Mears set out to create showmanship for his Wittenberg basketball program.

Mears started by having his players run through a large cutout of a Tiger when introduced. Lights were dimmed and the spotlight was on each player as he ran through to the roar of the crowd. He also used an entertaining warm-up routine to the strains of "Sweet Georgia Brown," as used by the Harlem Globetrotters, and brought in the highly acclaimed Dover Basketeers, who did a Globetrotter routine of their own during halftime at Wittenberg games. The group of young boys became so well-known that they were paid to perform in Jerry Lewis' "The Errand Boy" in 1961.

That was the same year Mears made good on his promise. He won the national title, beating Southeast Missouri, 42-38, in the championship game in Evansville, Indiana. The game's star was Don Wolfe, who had starred for Mears at West Tech in Cleveland and followed Mears to Wittenberg.

"He scored the last four points of the game and won the national championship for me," noted Mears.

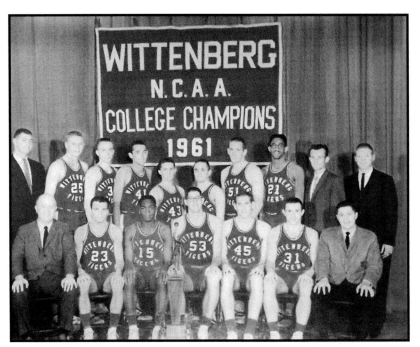

This is Ray Mears' 1961 Wittenberg National Championship Team. Mears is *seated, first row, on the right*.

Wolfe, though he'd starred for Mears at West Tech, was not recruited to Wittenberg by Mears. Rather, he walked on though he could have gotten a scholarship at any number of other schools.

"It was the first day of tryouts and I looked over and saw Wolfe," said Mears, "and I asked him what he was doing there."

Mears was surprised to see him because when Wolfe was a junior, Mears suspended him for two games in the middle of the season for drinking two beers at a wedding.

"I made him dress up in a suit and sit next to me those two games," said Mears. "After that year, I left and went to Wittenberg and he had a pretty good senior season."

Wolfe had come to Wittenberg to show his coach he could play for him and by his rules.

For a second chance with Mears, Wolfe's father borrowed money to send him to Wittenberg. Wolfe has since become a successful San Francisco businessman. When Wolfe was inducted into the Wittenberg Wall of Honor, he asked Mears to be his presenter.

"I told him he should have had Eldon Miller do it because he was his roommate in college and had coached at Ohio State all those years," said Mears. "But he said he wanted me to do that and I took that as a tremendous honor. Don Wolfe has more character than any player I ever coached."

Wolfe didn't score as many points in college as he did in high school, but played a key role in taking Wittenberg to the top.

The top player, however, was Terry Deems—a 6'4" forward—who was a holdover from the previous Wittenberg team. Deems established a host of scoring and rebounding records for Mears' teams at Wittenberg.

Mears' record his first year was 15-6. Records of 19-3, 19-3, 22-2, 24-4 and 21-5 followed. The Tigers won four Ohio Athletic Conference titles, enjoyed a 40-game winning streak at one point, and didn't lose a home game in the six years Mears was head coach. His winning percentage at Wittenberg was a sparkling .840 (121-23).

The calling card of Mears' teams was its stingy defense. His teams played a match-up zone that was designed to take away what the opponent liked to do best. It also allowed his post players to stay out of foul trouble. The Southeast Missouri team he beat to win the national title came in averaging nearly 90 points a game and got 38. Four of Mears' Wittenberg teams led the nation in defense and, later, two of his Tennessee teams would accomplish the same feat.

Mears also preached efficiency on offense, working for good shots in a time when he was not limited by a clock.

Deems saw the before/after contrast firsthand. He was at Wittenberg before Mears arrived and witnessed what the coach did to transform the Tigers from a sleepy perennial doormat in the Ohio Conference into a national championship team.

"Our team the year before was not very good," said Deems, who started as a freshman the previous year. "We were below .500. Few fans were coming to our games and we were having losing seasons. Wittenberg had never been that good."

But that all changed and changed in a hurry. Mears started by bringing in the pep band, the "Sweet Georgia Brown" routine, the Dover Basketeers and a pre-game show that included the players dunking the ball—something that was allowed in those days.

Mears coaching at Wittenberg in 1961-62.

"I think Coach Mears did his best job at Wittenberg," said Deems. "We were just a bunch of smart kids, but not the best basketball players in the world. He did it with his coaching style and with the entertainment that brought the fans in. We beat teams like Ohio, Dayton and Toledo and some of those teams had better players than we did at every position."

Deems was the first "star" in Mears' "Star System." Deems averaged 20 points and 17 rebounds per game for his career, including 20.4 rebounds per game as a junior.

Deems made All-Ohio Athletic Conference each of his three seasons and third-team All-American as a senior, making him Mears' first All-American. Other All-Americans under Mears at Wittenberg were Bert Price and George Fisher, while Al Thrasher—who was signed by Mears—earned All-American honors after Mears left for Tennessee.

Tony Wilcox, who went on to play for the Globetrotters, made All-Conference with Deems in 1958-59 and again in 1959-60. Tony Vedova was a second-team pick in 1958-59.

Price was All-Conference in 1959-60 and 1960-61. Wolfe was a second-team pick in 1960-61, when Wittenberg won the national title. And Thrasher and Fisher were all-league picks in Mears' final season, 1961-62. Thrasher made honorable mention All-American that year.

Another star was Miller, who went on to become head coach at Ohio State, a position he held for 10 years. He was team captain of the national championship team.

Mears' reputation allowed him to sign the top prospect in Ohio the following year, Thrasher, and two other starters from the Ohio-Indiana All-Star game.

So it was not out of the question that Mears could have also signed another All-Ohio star—Bobby Knight of Orrville, Ohio—a town famous for Smuckers' jellies.

"I was at Kent State one summer, taking some classes to work toward my masters degree," said Mears, "when I noticed this player by himself in the gym making shots from way out on the court. I asked him what his name was and he told me Bobby Knight.

"I asked him to visit Wittenberg and, to my surprise, he did."

It would have been illegal for Mears to watch Knight work out, but he had his players go work out with Knight and report back to him.

"They told me he wasn't good enough to play for Wittenberg," smiled Mears, noting that Knight signed with Ohio State, instead, and played on a national championship team there with Jerry Lucas and Don DeVoe, among others.

Knight, of course, went on to an outstanding coaching career of his own and won three national championships as head coach at Indiana before moving on to Texas Tech, where he became the all-time leader in coaching victories during the 2007 season. He won NCAA titles, an NIT title (1979) and an Olympic title as a head coach. Mears and Knight remained friends for years and what happened during Mears' recruitment of Knight was often a topic of discussion.

"Every time I talk with him, he reminds me that I didn't offer him a scholarship," said Mears. "I'll always remember that when I was forced to resign (in 1978), because of my health, he was the first coach to call me and see if there was anything he could do for me. But that's Bobby Knight. Everywhere he goes, he inspires great loyalty."

**Mears (*right*) with Boston Celtic great, Bob Cousy (*left*) and
Bobby Knight in Madison Square Garden. Mears recruited Knight out of high school.**

Chapter 4

A Clandestine Coach Search

W hen Wittenberg won the 1961 small college national title and looked like it might do it again, *Sports Illustrated* came calling and wrote a story on the young coach that was part of the February 26, 1962 issue.

Jim McDonald, one of Bowden Wyatt's top assistants on the football team at Tennessee at the time, was from Springfield, Ohio and brought the article to the attention of his boss, who was Acting Athletic Director at the time.

With Tennessee's basketball team struggling to a 4-19 season, it was obvious a change had to be made. But with General Bob Neyland, the athletic director at the time, on his death bed any search for a new coach would have to be a clandestine operation. John Sines, who had been a member of Neyland's football staff in the 1950s, was the head basketball coach and Neyland would never agree to dismiss him because of his loyalty to Sines.

With Neyland's death imminent, however, Wyatt gave McDonald the go-ahead to contact Mears and bring him to Knoxville for an interview.

"Jim was one of Bowden's closest friends and since he'd coached in Springfield, he knew about me," said Mears. "He was quite a player at Ohio State and had been captain of the football and basketball teams. He was a great athlete."

In late March of 1962, when Mears' team was in the nationals in Evansville, Indiana, McDonald called. After Mears' team was eliminated from the tournament by Mt. Saint Mary's, Mears and wife Dana got on a plane for Knoxville while his team went back to Wittenberg.

Mears and his wife were put up in the fanciest hotel in town—the Andrew Johnson.

"They put us up in the Governor's Suite and brought in all of our food," said Mears. "We never toured the campus and later I learned it was because they were afraid someone would recognize me and word would get out that they were looking for a new basketball coach, though an opening didn't exist.

"When Bowden came up, he had a little too much to drink and was loud. He kind of looked like John Wayne. He kind of scared me. I thought: 'Lord, what is this'?"

Wyatt never told Mears the job was not open, but took him in one of the bedrooms for an interview and asked him how much money it would take to get him to Knoxville. Mears had started at Wittenberg at $5,000 a year and had gotten token raises of about $150 per season over six years.

"I basically asked for double what I was making at Wittenberg or $11,500," said Mears. "He said, 'Fine.' Then he told me that I could have as many scholarships as I needed to get the job done. He told me they didn't do contracts at Tennessee; they just did handshakes. I said, 'okay.'"

Mears didn't hear anything more for a couple weeks and flirted with a job at Denver University at the time. But the Tennessee job was the one he wanted. Finally, Mears was officially named Tennessee's eleventh head basketball coach on April 19, 1962, following Sines' dismissal.

Neyland passed away on March 28, 1962, and never knew of Mears' hiring or Sines' dismissal.

John Sines

Chapter 5

Putting the Blocks in Place

Mears hired a young assistant who was coaching high school ball in Ohio, Bill Gibbs. Like Mears, he was a Miami of Ohio grad, and together they started the recruiting process.

The NCAA had not set any scholarship limits at the time and Mears took advantage of Wyatt's generous offer to sign 18 players, bringing his roster to 26 players.

Included in those he signed were two players who his freshmen teams at Wittenberg had played against in scrimmages. They were members of an Industrial League team in Dayton, Ohio. Howard Bayne was 6'5" and a Tarzan clone. Larry McIntosh was a 6'2" guard. Both were twenty-two-years old and had no intention of going to college before Mears called.

"Gibbs suggested we go up and get those guys," said Mears, adding: "I don't know how we got them into school."

Bayne, who hadn't graduated from high school, did the work necessary to get a GED. Each started all three years of their eligibility.

"Bayne had moves like Ernie Grunfeld and I really liked Larry McIntosh," said Mears. "He came even though he was married."

Others in that recruiting class were Red Robbins, a JC player from Chipola, Florida, who became an All-American, and JC player Jimmy Cornwall, who became a starter and a solid player.

Mears was blessed, too, in that the cupboard was not left bare by Sines—though his team had finished dead last in the 12-team SEC his final season.

"The team had a 4-19 record the year before," said Mears in an interview with Tom Mattingly of *Smokey's Tale*, a magazine once produced by the Tennessee Sports Information office, "which meant there was hardly any direction to go but up. And also, John Sines had left me some remarkable young material. A.W. Davis was coming into his sophomore year, Danny Schultz had been recruited from Hiwassee Junior College and there were fellows like Pat Robinette and Bobby Hogsett coming up."

UT Sports Information

This photograph of Mears was taken in 1962 during his first year at Tennessee.

Added Mears: "No one told me the freshmen were that good, but they had actually beaten the varsity several times."

Davis was from nearby Rutledge and Hogsett from Holston Valley near Bristol. Both were heavily recruited the year before. Robinette was from Bristol, Virginia. There was also a group that included Jerry Parker, Orb Bowling, Tommy Wilson and Sid Elliott—all starters—who were returning.

Sid Elliott (54) is fouled by a Phillips 66 Oilers player in 1962-63 exhibition game; A. W. Davis (20) looks on. Mears' health problems benched him for most of that season.

Mears said Davis was a key to the Tennessee turnaround, even though Schultz made the most immediate impact and wound up being the first Tennessee All-American under Mears.

"I give A.W. credit for coming," said Mears. "He could have gone to Kentucky. He was the number-one player Adolph Rupp wanted. But he wanted to help build Tennessee's program."

The Rutledge Rifle helped put Tennessee on the map with three wonderful seasons and then later helped coach on the sidelines with Mears for several years.

It's important to note that before Mears' arrival, Tennessee has lost 22 of its previous 23 games with Kentucky. That was about to change.

Mears in his office.

Chapter 6

The Rutledge Rifle

Kentucky was hot and heavy in pursuit of A.W. Davis when Tennessee was able to sign him the year before Mears arrived.

"When I was a sophomore in high school," relates Davis, "Kentucky was the first school I heard from."

Then, when Davis set the state scoring record as a senior, the "Rutledge Rifle" was presented the game ball by Kentucky assistant Harry Lancaster.

"Coach (Adolph) Rupp even came to my school to help recruit me," noted Davis, "and it was my understanding that that didn't happen a lot."

But fate intervened. As Davis, his parents and his high school coach were heading to Lexington for his Kentucky visit, there was a "heckuva" snowstorm that caused them to turn around after getting as far as Corbin, Kentucky.

Davis never made it to Lexington. He did visit Vanderbilt and liked coach Bob Polk, but Polk confessed to him late that season on a visit to Knoxville to play Tennessee that this would be his last year.

"He had a heart condition that was going to cause him to quit," said Davis.

He also visited Florida, where Norm Sloan was coach.

But Andy Holt, the Tennessee president, won him over with an act of kindness.

"I was to meet Dr. Holt on my campus visit," said Davis. "He was my host. He was driving me around and showing me all of the buildings when there came a pouring rain. There were two students on the corner, caught in the rain, and Dr. Holt stopped and told them to "get in here." He asked them where they were going and dropped them off at their next class. I thought that was pretty neat for a president to do something like that. That made a big impression on me and Tennessee was my last visit."

With Davis the star in a star-studded freshman class, it often beat the varsity, which finished 4-19 his freshman year when he and others weren't eligible.

A. W. Davis was one of Mears' first stars.

"Some people came to see the freshman game, then left," said Davis, who said the freshmen split with Kentucky and Vanderbilt and swept Georgia Tech in its six games.

When Sines learned he wouldn't be retained, the first person he called was Davis.

"I liked Coach Sines and thought he did a very good job recruiting me," said Davis.

Davis didn't know anything about Mears, but was impressed from the first meeting. Mears came to Rutledge to meet with Davis and his family. He was also impressed with the first team meeting.

"He spoke to us about how it was going to be and afterwards, some of the older guys who had been through that 4-19 season said 'Hey. We can win!'"

Davis said they realized "he was something special" at that first meeting. "What you'd see in the course of a season was that he'd never ask you to do more than he was willing to do himself."

They did, sweeping Kentucky twice Mears' first season though Mears wasn't there for most of it. He became ill on a trip to El Paso and had to leave the team in the hands of assistant Bill Gibbs.

"Coach Gibbs did an okay job," said Davis. "I think the highlight of my sophomore year came when we were playing Kentucky in Lexington and we were down 16 points at halftime. Before leaving the locker room, he wrote on the chalk board: *You can, if you think you can.* We then went out and won the game. We also beat them in Knoxville later on for a sweep."

In 1965, his senior year, Davis was honored as Tennessee's second basketball All-American. Danny Schultz had become the first under Mears in 1964. Davis averaged 14.9, 17.3 and then 19.6 in his three seasons at Tennessee. He was drafted by the Los Angeles Lakers.

"But I chose not to go. I wanted to coach, instead, and spent a year as a graduate assistant under Coach Mears and then went to McMinn Central as the head coach. In my second year there, I was drafted by the Kentucky Colonels of the ABA and signed with them. I played for ten weeks before suffering a back injury and that was it."

Davis returned to coach with Mears as a full-time assistant from 1969 through 1975.

One of Davis' favorite memories of his days with Mears came in a game at Kentucky.

"One of the officials was obviously drunk and Coach Rupp came over to Ray and said 'You know Jim's about drunk. I don't know what we're going to do.' Then Coach Rupp told Ray that there was an official up in the stands who had officiated some local games and suggested they have him help work the game.

"Mears looked at Rupp and said: 'I'll take my chances on Jim!'"

Added Davis: "The guy went on to work the best game I've ever seen. When Coach Mears got into a game situation, it was like war. He'd do anything he could to win."

Left to right, **Wayne Tomlinson,
Eddie Voelker and Coach Mears.**

Chapter 7

Showtime

Before Mears arrived, only 400 fans had turned out for Tennessee's final regular-season home game against Tulane. From a fan-interest standpoint, the program was dead.

That made the tactics Mears had used at Wittenberg most welcome. The Globetrotter-like dribbling routines, the use of "Sweet Georgia Brown" and "Tiger Rag," and players running through a tigers' mouth when introduced were all part of it.

Wittenberg player runs through a tiger's mouth.

Instead of a tigers' mouth, Tennessee's basketball players started running on the court through a large, cut-out 'T'—something that later became a tradition for the football team, as well. Mears also had a brass band march into the building, led by twirling majorettes, and march around the court to create a festive atmosphere.

UT Sports Information

UT paper mache 'T'—the origin of "Running through the 'T'" for UT athletes.

Quickly, Mears had the fans on their feet clapping.

The ploy had worked at Wittenberg, where his teams won 69 straight home games.

"The idea was to intimidate our opponent," said Mears. "That was part of my coaching strategy. You can't always win on talent alone."

"It's psychological warfare," said former Buffalo coach Len Serfustini in Mears' coaching notebook published in the 1970 to share his philosophies with other college coaches. His team lost to Mears and Tennessee in 1964, 79-54.

"I give Ray Mears credit for excellent planning. He had our boys pretty well over-awed before the tipoff. That stuff is intimidating and when you get the other team worried before the game even starts, you're halfway home."

"When you played at Tennessee, you thought you were under the big top," LSU's Brown told the *Nashville Tennessean* after Mears' death. "I remember coming onto the court to warm up and their band was right under our basket with these great big tubas.

"I walked over and said: 'Coach Mears, you're going to have to move the band.' He said he didn't think he would. Then I said, 'Well, you'd better find out what one of those tubas costs because you're going to have to buy a new one after one of my players runs right over that guy playing it.'

"He kind of laughed and got the band to step out of the way."

Added Brown: "Back at a time when the league needed to promote basketball, Ray Mears was a promoter. He had one of the best promotional minds in the profession. I stole a lot of his ideas.

"It was a spectacle when you went to Knoxville to play."

Mears later had someone wrestle a bear between games of the Volunteer Classic. In 1971, before games, he had Roger Peltz, one of his players, ride a unicycle and juggle balls at the same time.

"He wasn't going to help us much with his play, so his full-time job with the team became riding the unicycle and performing," said Mears. "It helped that he was a comedian. That became his career."

Fans started coming to the game a half hour ahead of tip-off to take in Mears' "Showtime."

Roger Peltz was a reserve player, whose talents Mears used as part of his "Showtime" routine—juggling basketballs while riding a unicycle.

UT Sports Information

Mears said his gimmicks, which he learned from watching Bill Veeck promote the Cleveland Indians with all kinds of special activities, served another purpose.

"Back then, we played a slow-paced game and our games were low-scoring," said Mears. "So we had to give them another reason to come."

Mears said that Veeck gave him the idea to be a promoter.

"He might have been the first one to have a free give-away at a game," said Mears. "Now you see that all the time at baseball games. He made tickets inexpensive so everyone could come to games and got a lot of the blue-collar workers coming to games."

Mears started the Volunteer Classic, when Stokely Center was opened, and planned special entertainment between games.

One of his promotions was to bring in a wrestling bear from Cherokee, N.C.

"Marty Morris (Mears' special assistant) set up a parade through town where the bear rode down Gay Street in the back of a white Volkswagen convertible with orange fenders. It got people interested in coming to the game," said Mears. "I was constantly trying to help get people out."

Mears said Morris and the trainer also took the bear into a Knoxville bar where it sat on a stool and drank a beer.

At the game, Mears hoped to get UT Orange Tie Club president Jim Haslam to wrestle the bear, but he declined. Peltz tackled the bear from his unicycle and almost got suffocated when it rolled on top of him. Fortunately, the bear had been de-teethed and de-clawed and was gentle by nature.

"John Paschal (a health club owner) put a bear hug on him and the bear backed up and ran away," said Mears. "Those were the only two who would wrestle the bear. It was probably the funniest thing we ever did."

That particular incident was typical of the kind of gimmicks Mears used to draw fans.

From the beginning, they started to come in droves and it didn't take long for the size of the crowds to make it necessary to expand the Armory-Fieldhouse, which seated 7,500, into Stokely Center that opened in time for the 1966-67 SEC Championship season.

In addition to intimidating opponents with his pre-game gimmicks, Mears' coaching philosophy was to frustrate his opponent any other way possible.

"Whatever you do, I try to do the opposite," said Mears in his basketball notebook. "About 85 percent of the college coaches have the same basic philosophy on basketball. I'm in the other 15 percent."

Mears would begin practices by talking about life to his players for as long as a half hour.

Lloyd Richardson also took
his turn at juggling basketballs.

"My philosophy of coaching is based on the same characteristics needed to wage a victorious battle against life's problems," wrote Mears in his basketball notebook. "Opportunity for advancement doesn't present itself often; therefore, one aim in coaching is to prepare the boys to recognize opportunity when it comes and make sure it doesn't pass them by.

"I feel that a basketball game is like a chess match. The team that makes the most intelligent moves will win. In a situation where our personnel is weak, I teach the boys to do the unorthodox. If the team likes to fast break and is an excellent driving team, I instruct my team to attempt to slow the tempo of the game by playing a controlled game. We may change our style of play a number of times in attempting to find the formula needed to stop that club. I feel that the players will be better able to cope with life's problems after working with this type of play."

Mears said there's lots of room in this world for a winner, but the "Standing Room Only" sign is for losers.

"In life, you are always fighting to get ahead so you must develop a winning spirit. I insist that a boy have this winning spirit, and that he keeps winning uppermost in his mind," wrote Mears. "Even with this winning spirit, it must be remembered that victory is a means to an end and not the end itself.

"I teach the boys to be humble winners and gracious, but hard losers. A 'gracious, but hard loser' is one who takes defeat graciously, but hates to lose. I feel that a hard loser, who suffers an occasional defeat, will profit by that defeat. He will think and talk over the cause of defeat and will make sure that same cause never defeats him again."

Mears' theory was that most losses went to the team that made the most mistakes and stressed the difference between intelligent mistakes and wild mistakes.

"An intelligent mistake is one where the player makes the correct maneuver, but fails to carry out the play because of some unforseen circumstance. This type of mistake, we forgive but work to eliminate. A wild mistake is an attempt to do some act the player should never have tried in the first place. This one, we do not condone; even if it is successful."

Mears said he'd rather have a player with a burning spirit than one without spirit who had great natural ability. He said it was his job to exhibit the kind of spirit he wanted his players to have.

"I feel the coach should be a living example of enthusiasm—even more than his most ardent player," wrote Mears. "As Emerson said: 'Nothing great was ever achieved without enthusiasm.'"

Chapter 8

A Scary Beginning

Though Mears quickly got the show on the road when he arrived in 1962, all was not well.

The Mears Era almost didn't get off the ground. Mears had never had any emotional problems before arriving in Knoxville, but in the summer before his first season in 1962, the 35-year-old coach suddenly started having problems. He was later diagnosed as being manic depressive—a chemical imbalance, but at the time little was known about the disorder and the diagnosis was unclear.

"It was my son's birthday, at the end of July, and Jim McDonald took me to the bicycle shop," said Mears. "I began to feel faint. I had never been hospitalized or even sick in my 35 years. Jim took me to the hospital and they gave me a tranquilizer. After that, I couldn't sleep. I got insomnia and it got to where I couldn't sleep for more than a half-hour or an hour at a time. I would watch TV and nonsense would come out. It was terrible. It took a long time to get it worked out."

Mears started trying to coach the team, but was disoriented and Wyatt sent him to Florida with his family for rest and relaxation while Gibbs coached the first two games. Mears returned for the next four games, but then started having problems again.

"After a game against Texas Western in El Paso, they said I was completely out of it," said Mears. "They think I had a nervous breakdown. I didn't know where I was after the game."

This time, Mears was sent to a mental hospital in Radford, Virginia.

"At first, they put me in a ward with patients who were considered dangerous," said Mears. "I didn't know who I was, but I remember it as the worst experience in my life. It was a wonder I got out of there alive, though no one ever attacked me. After two days, they put me in a regular ward."

The decision was then made to use electric shock therapy.

"I had it eight-to-ten times," said Mears. "They did it two or three times a week. They'd put something in my mouth to bite down on, then would give me a shot to put me to sleep. I would pass out. I never felt it."

Added Mears: "It's not like the Jack Nicholson movie (*One Flew Over The Cuckoos' Nest*). Electric shock just sounds bad. The doctors at Radford believed in them and I completely got over it."

Mears returned to the team with two games left in the season, but let Gibbs finish out coaching.

"I didn't have any more problems until 1977," said Mears. "I had some bad days where I didn't feel good. They didn't have the medicine that they do today or I would have been coaching a long time."

That first Mears' team went 13-11 overall and 6-8 in the SEC, finishing seventh. It did, however, beat Kentucky twice and more than tripled its number of wins from the previous season, giving fans hope for the future of the program.

Davis said the team was concerned when Mears fell ill, "because everyone on the team really liked and respected Coach Mears."

Mears said the stresses of his situation likely set off his problems. Not long after he'd been hired, Wyatt called him to his house to introduce him to Tommy Bartlett—captain of the 1952 Tennessee basketball team—who the AD said would be one of his assistant coaches. He'd been head coach at UT-Chattanooga.

"He said I needed a freshman coach," said Mears. "I didn't like it because I didn't know what I was getting. But Tommy called his president right there and said he was going to take the job up here."

Bowden Wyatt

Mears said that he thought the move to put Bartlett on the staff came about because his own hiring had rankled some supporters who were upset that Bartlett had not also been interviewed for the job and this was the way to appease them.

This was Mears' team in 1963-64 when he coached his first full season. Members were: *Kneeling front row, left to right*; **Coach Jerry Parker, Coach Bill Gibbs, Mears and Coach Tommy Bartlett.** *Second row, left to right*; **Manager Barry Bundrant, Jim Finley, Larry McIntosh, Skip Plotnicki, Pat Robinette, Danny Neff, Jimmy Crone, Danny Schultz, Manager Rob Sandford.** *Back row, left to right*; **Joe Pietropola, Gil Monroe, Howard Bayne, John Jacobs, Bobby Hogsett, A. W. Davis, Sid Elliott and Rick Keebler.**

"I think there was pressure put on Bowden to give Tommy a job," said Mears. "That caused a mental concern for me. I thought they might be trying to edge me out then.

"This was unusual, because at that time most schools only had one assistant coach. But Tommy did a good job for me and was very loyal."

Bartlett used his position at Tennessee as a stepping stone to the Florida head coaching job, which he held from 1967 to 1973. One of his stars was Neal Walk.

Bartlett likely would have taken over for Mears, had he not been able to continue in 1962, though some thought Gibbs would get the job if Mears didn't come back.

Gibbs had beaten Kentucky twice, but something he did didn't sit well with the players or Mears, when he learned of it.

"People liked him because he'd beaten Kentucky twice, but he lost some games he shouldn't have and after a loss at Tulane, rather than take the players out for a meal after the game, he put milk and donuts outside their rooms," said Mears. "A.W. Davis said the players were really upset about it. He did it a couple of times and I don't think he would have gotten the job, if I hadn't come back."

Gibbs was tragically killed in a crash of a light plane carrying nine passengers while on his way from Gainesville, Fla., to Auburn, Ala., on February 3, 1964 to scout Auburn. According to reports, the plane lifted no more than 100 feet off the ground on takeoff.

To honor the fallen assistant, Tennessee named Gibbs Hall, the athletic dorm, in his honor.

A young head coach
Ray Mears in a casual moment.

Chapter 9

The Orange Tie Club

Always the promoter, Mears looked for a way to get fans to wear Tennessee's orange colors at games.

The idea for wearing the colors of the team came from Mears' experience while he was at Wittenberg. It came from a rival, the Evansville Aces in basketball-crazy Indiana.

"They got the NCAA to play the small-college championship at Evansville, Indiana," said Mears. "They played in Roberts Memorial, which was a big place for Division II back then.

"Evansville had like 9,000 fans then who all wore the same (maroon) color and they tore that place apart. You couldn't hear yourself think. I thought that this was the sort of thing I needed to do."

So when some interested fans came to Mears and asked what they could do to help out, he was ready with a proposal.

"I suggested they start an Orange Tie Club," said Mears. "We'd never had orange in the place and this was a way we could get it at the games."

Hank Bertlekamp, a former Tennessee basketball captain and now a prominent businessman in Knoxville (and father of current Tennessee Basketball Analyst and former player Bert Bertlekamp), and dentist Earl Keister got together with Mears and followed up on his idea to develop the club. Current Pilot Oil Company CEO Jim Haslam was also a prominent member of the Orange Tie Club and later became its president.

They acquired orange ties for approximately 100 members of the club who would sit together at games. Later, membership swelled to as many as 500.

"I don't know where they got them, but they got them," said Mears. "They had orange ties that we'd put in the cloakroom and have the guys put them on when they came to games. They'd wear white shirts and you'd look up and see that splash of orange. It was the first splash of orange at a Tennessee game."

Former Tennessee president Edward J. Boling backs up Mears' claim.

"Ray's the one who started the use of the colors," said Boling, "as I recall it. I don't remember anything being done before that. He had the Orange Tie Club and had them sit in a special section. He also put orange blazers on his players. Before Ray's time, we were just a hard-nosed football school."

Mears also liked the North Carolina sky blue color and used it as trim on his orange uniforms.

"A lot of fans complained about it because Tennessee's colors since 1890 had been orange and white," said Mears. "But I liked it. Pat Summitt (Lady Vols' head coach) still uses it."

**Former University of Tennessee
President, Dr. Edward J. Boling**

Chapter 10

This is Big Orange Country

Taking the Orange Tie Club idea a step further, Mears decided to put his players in orange blazers that they'd wear while traveling. He also had orange blazers made for his coaching staff.

Mears got some negative feedback from his players at first, because no one wore bright colors in those days. Some of the players told Mears they looked like a band. His reply: "You've got to have a little pride in your school."

"I was embarrassed," admitted Howard Bayne. "Everywhere we went, people would stare at us. It was as though we were a circus act. But, in time, I became very proud of it."

Today, such apparel is easy to come by. But in those days, there were none to be found in stores in Knoxville.

"I had to go to Mississippi to order white cloth from the mills down there and have them dyed orange," said Mears. "All they had around here were black, brown or charcoal."

The blazers and the Orange Tie Club started the craze at Tennessee, but it got a major boost in the late 1960s when Mears got an idea that would revolutionize the Tennessee sports scene.

"After I came, people were starting to wear orange," said Mears. "One day, after I'd seen the sign for about the millionth time, an idea hit me. It was the sign from Marlboro Country. I thought: *Why not Big Orange Country?*"

The idea stuck.

The idea of "Big Orange" came from his experience in Ohio. He had witnessed the use of the "Big Red" slogan that fans identified with Steubenville, Ohio. It was a name that became synonymous with the high school that was famous for its football tradition.

"In Ohio, there were 40 teams that wore red," said Mears, "but only Steubenville had been known as the 'Big Red.'"

Bayne said he vividly recalls the day Mears first told him of his idea.

"We were on a trip to Mississippi when we passed the Marlboro Country sign," said Bayne. "I told him 'Coach, we should call it Volunteer Country.' But he said he already had it planned out. He said we were going to be 'Big Orange Country.' I think John Ward and Marvin West (*Knoxville News-Sentinel* sports writer) were sitting right there when we had that conversation."

To market his idea, Mears got help from Tom Rechenbach, who owned a book store in Knoxville in 1965. Like the Marlboro Country billboards, Mears used "This is Big Orange Country" billboards to promote his basketball team. Rechenbach produced sweatshirts, tee shirts, window stickers, belts and other items that are taken for granted by Tennessee fans today.

"He was outstanding," said Ward, long time "Voice of the Vols" of Mears' knack for promotion. "The basic thing about Ray is he was the right man at the right time because he could not only coach basketball and recruit quality players, but he could market the product. If I recall, when he first came, Tennessee had sold just 900 season tickets. He had a tremendous job to do.

"What he did was create an atmosphere and deliver a product that was saleable. And he created an ethic that transcended basketball. It became a vital part of Tennessee's overall marketing. People say he's a great marketer. People think of just basketball, but it was total athletic marketing. I'm talking 'Big Orange' ... The concept of wearing orange coats and ties to the game. He created an atmosphere. While he could coach and do all that, to my mind, he was first a marketer."

One of Mears' ideas that has become a part of Tennessee tradition is the way Tennessee's football team runs through the 'T' formed by the marching band at football games.

"Doug Dickey (Vol football coach in the 1960s) was involved in having the team running through the 'T,' but running through the 'T' came from Mears in basketball, having his players run through the wooden 'T,'" said Ward.

Today, Tennessee fans come to football and basketball games in Knoxville and on the road decked out in their orange clothes and Knoxville is known by the monicker Mears gave the city—it is and all of East Tennessee is, truly, **"Big Orange Country."**

**Marlboro Man Billboard ad that gave
Coach Mears the "Big Orange Country" idea.**

**Mears and his players getting off plane donated by
Mason-Dixon of Kingsport. Mears had the jackets shipped
from Mississippi. They were dyed orange in Knoxville.**

**Mears with the help of Tom Rechenbach used
"Big Orange Country" billboards to promote his basketball program. It wasn't
long before the idea caught on and was also used to help promote Tennessee football.**

Chapter 11

The Kentucky Challenge

When Mears first arrived in Knoxville, Tom Siler, who was the *News-Sentinel* sports editor, wrote that his task was to beat Kentucky, the perennial powerhouse in the Southeastern Conference. Mears took the challenge seriously.

Knoxville News-Sentinel **sports editor Tom Siler challenged Mears to stand up to Adolph Rupp and his Kentucky Wildcats.**

In his 15 years as Tennessee's head coach, his team broke even against Kentucky, posting a 15-15 record overall. Against the legendary Adolph Rupp, that record was 8-12, but some of the losses Mears put on Rupp were especially distasteful to the "Baron of the Bluegrass."

Mears' 1966 team ruined Kentucky's perfect regular season with a 69-62 upset of "Rupp's Runts" in a year they'd finish as NCAA runner-up, and in 1968 his team handed Rupp his worst-ever SEC defeat—an 87-59 setback in Knoxville.

Mears' game plan against Rupp was to find a way to upset him so he wouldn't coach his best against Tennessee.

"Rupp was superior to me," said Mears. "So I'd try to get him a little edgy so he wouldn't coach as well. I'd try to gig him."

Rupp was always decked out in his famous brown suit. It was to Rupp what the houndstooth hat was to Alabama football coach Bear Bryant.

Ray Mears, in his orange jacket, shakes hands with Adolph Rupp in his traditional brown suit. Mears crossed the line one night and donned a brown suit, sending Rupp into a rage behind closed doors.

"He always wore his brown suit and I always wore my orange blazer," said Mears. "But one day, I went out and bought a cheap brown suit for $15. That night, I wore it at the game in Lexington.

"He comes over to shake hands and he looks at me. I said: 'Coach, what do you think of my brown suit? I wore it just for you.' He said 'Christ!' and just turned and walked off. I thought he'd get madder."

But the ploy had its desired effect.

"A trainer for Kentucky told me later that he went back to the locker room and started kicking chairs and yelling: 'There's only one man in this country worthy of wearing a brown suit to coach in and Mears ought to know that!,'" Mears recalled with a chuckle.

Added Mears: "We didn't win that night, but we won some others."

"It took a certain amount of brashness," said former *Knoxville Journal Sports* Editor Ben Byrd in a *Smokey's Tale* article in 1987, referring to Mears' approach to Rupp, "maybe even a bit of arrogance to take Rupp on at a time when he had things pretty much his way. Ray deliberately rubbed Rupp the wrong way.

Adolph Rupp. Mears didn't feel he could outcoach Rupp, so he tried to get under his skin.

"Rupp wanted to use the physical advantage his teams had. Mears' slow-paced style rubbed Rupp the wrong way.

"It was a battle of egos as much as philosophies. They were alike in an overwhelming desire to win, to excel. They just used different tactics to get there. Rupp probably didn't really like Mears until after he retired. He didn't like anybody who challenged his supremacy at the time."

For the upset of "Rupp's Runts," Mears got an assist from the Tennessee football team.

"The football players were good friends with our basketball players because they stayed in the athletic dorm and ate meals together," said Mears. "So when Kentucky came in here unbeaten (23-0), about 30 of the football players came in behind Rupp's bench and they rode him all night. Rupp couldn't handle it. He had rabbit ears and they were on him the whole game.

"We got off to about a 20-point lead, then they came back within five points and at that point, I didn't know if we'd beat them or not. But we wound up winning by seven (69-62). After the game, the football players raced onto the court and carried the basketball players off. It was spontaneous. I don't think anyone had done that before or since."

UT Sports Information

Mears and Tommy Bartlett dry off after taking a "shower" following their upset of Rupps Runts in 1966. It was the Wildcats' only regular-season loss. Kentucky later lost to Texas Western in the National Championship finals.

Howard Bayne, a senior playing in his last game, didn't consider the upset an upset.

"I thought we had the better team," said Bayne.

Later on, Bayne became friends with several members of that team, including Larry Conley and Louie Dampier, playing with Dampier on the Kentucky Colonels of the ABA after both were out of school. Cotton Nash, an earlier Kentucky star, also played with Bayne on the Colonels.

Bayne said that win over Kentucky was especially meaningful to him because he had been forced to miss several games before that with an injury.

Mears always respected Rupp and said people would be surprised at how good their relationship was off the court in those days.

"He spoke at our banquet twice," said Mears in the 1987 *Smokey's Tale* article. "One of the great things in my life was getting to play against several of his best teams."

Mears posted a 7-3 record against Rupp's successor, Joe B. Hall, and five of those victories came after an incident in which Vol star freshman Bernard King was burned on the head and back by a lighted cigarette that was flipped at him as the Vols were coming off the floor following an 88-82 loss in Lexington in 1975.

"I was right behind him when it happened," said Rodney Woods, the point guard on the team at the time. "We were going under the walkway when the cigarette hit him and burned a hole in the back of his jersey. He ran toward the bleachers after the guy and Coach (Stu) Aberdeen ran after him. The coaches grabbed him and escorted him to the locker room."

But the incident brought about a pledge from King, who is still regarded as Tennessee's all-time best player and one of the SEC's all-time best.

"After the cooling-off period, they let the media in to talk with us and Bernard stuck his finger in the chest of a Kentucky writer and told him that Kentucky would never again beat Tennessee while he was in Tennessee uniform," said Woods.

King made good on his pledge. Tennessee won the next five games it played against Kentucky, starting with a 103-98 victory in Knoxville later that season, then sweeping the Wildcats the next two seasons. In the game in Lexington in 1976, King made a shot from almost flat on his back that proved a key play in a 90-88 overtime victory. Later that season in Knoxville, the Vols won 92-85. In the 1976-77 season, they beat Kentucky in Lexington again, 71-67 in overtime, and followed with an 81-79 victory in Knoxville that put the Vols in position to tie for the SEC title.

Woods, who played from 1973-75 and served as captain of the 1975 team, especially relished beating Kentucky. Tennessee finished 3-3 against the Wildcats during his career.

"Every boy in the state of Kentucky grows up dreaming of playing for the Wildcats, and I was no exception," said Woods, who was from Four Mile, Kentucky, near Middlesboro. "My first cousin had been a starter in his sophomore year at Kentucky in 1959, so I got to go to some games, which caused me to want to wear the blue even more.

"During my senior season, Kentucky coaches watched me play twice and I had a visit, dinner on Saturday night with Joe B. Hall and breakfast on Saturday morning with Coach Rupp. But, in the meantime, the Tennessee coaches saw me play 17 consecutive times and my father told me one night that he would go where I was wanted the most. When I announced I would attend Tennessee, the Kentucky coaches called and asked me to hold off until they could come in and make another pitch, but I declined because I was sold on Tennessee because of Ray Mears."

Woods said he seemed to get closer to Mears than any of the other players.

"Coach Mears knew I wanted to be a coach," said Woods, who is now one of the top high school coaches in Kentucky, "and sometimes I believe that is one of the reasons he was always teaching me about why he was making certain decisions. Also, he knew after three years, that I would walk across broken glass barefoot for him or the 'Big Orange.'

"I think he had a lot of confidence in me because many times he would call me in when someone had broken a team rule or was displaying an attitude that was hurting the team and ask what I thought he should do. We didn't always agree, but I really feel that most of the time he made the decision that I would be for because I think he knew that I really knew the team. After three years, I probably thought as much like him as anyone. He used to say at banquets that one of the reasons we got along so well was that I was the one guy he knew who felt the same way about Kentucky as he did."

One thing Mears is most proud of is the comment Rupp made from his wheel chair in 1977 while he was retired.

"Ray Mears is the best basketball coach in America," said Rupp, who was replaced by Mears on the "Winningest Active Coach" list after both he and UCLA's John Wooden retired. Dean Smith of North Carolina passed Mears on the list the following season.

Chapter 12

Gigging Vanderbilt

Mears always tried to get the best of his opponent, whether it was at home or on the road. But his way of getting under the skin of Vanderbilt Commodore fans actually came about by accident.

Ward, who broadcast Tennessee basketball games and did the Ray Mears' basketball show before ever doing Tennessee football, was with Mears when the famous "Vanderbilt Walk" first took place.

The "Vanderbilt Walk" came on March 3, 1969 and was continued by Mears until he was finally ordered by SEC Commissioner Tonto Coleman to stop intimidating Vanderbilt fans with it and other gimmicks in 1972.

"I was sitting with Ray watching the freshman game," said Ward, who retired from broadcasting in 1999. "We were at one end of the court and one of the ushers came up and told Ray that they'd moved the dressing room to the other end of the floor.

"Near the end of the first half, Ray told the team: 'Let's go to the dressing room.' Now Memorial Gym is like the catacombs underneath, so rather than walk all the way back, we just walked down the court. It was the shortest distance between two points—a straight line. But the Vandy fans thought Ray had done it on purpose to irritate them. Once they reacted, he got to the other end of the court, turned to me and said: "I've got 'em."

"I think the thing that really angered them is I had the boys take off their overcoats and show their orange jackets as they walked," said Mears. "I think that's the thing that really upset the Vanderbilt fans. It was the first time we'd worn them there."

Tennessee's players, underdogs going in, fed off the crowd reaction. First, the freshmen rallied to win their game, then Mears' varsity pulled a 70-60 upset over the favored Commodores.

"Every game from then on out, he'd walk the length of the floor and the Vandy fans would howl," said Ward. "It's not that he planned it that first time. It's because the Vanderbilt fans reacted the way they did that he kept on doing it."

Then-assistant A.W. Davis said he played a role in Mears' famous walk at Vanderbilt.

While Mears claimed it was an accident that worked out in Tennessee's favor, Davis said it was no accident. Davis was coaching the JV team that, at the time, played the game before the varsity played.

"He told me when I saw him at the end of the gym, to call a timeout," said Davis. "I said 'What if I don't need a timeout?' He told me, 'If you want your job, you'll call a timeout when you see me.'"

Davis said they moved the Tennessee locker room to prevent Mears from putting on a show, but that Mears intentionally positioned himself and the varsity players to take their historic trip across the middle of the floor to enrage the Vanderbilt fans.

Mears, the next year, got the 6'8", 250-pound Bill Skinner, who was a javelin champion, to walk with him as a bodyguard. Skinner had been a bouncer at a bar and was fearless. During pre-game warm-ups, Vandy fans captured Tennessee's orange-and-white practice ball and starting tossing it around the stands. Skinner, however, went up into the bleachers full of Vandy students and retrieved the ball without incident.

"That shook me up," admitted Mears, who always did the walk without the team after that first time. "If they had decided to gang up on Bill, he wouldn't have had a chance."

Mears said Skinner's reaction, when he asked him to be his personal bodyguard at the game was: "Do you want me to bring my gun?" After all, there had been threats on Mears' life if he did the walk. That's why he asked Skinner to accompany him.

Mears said, "Skinner wore former star Tom Boerwinkle's orange blazer. It's the only one that would fit him."

Billy Justus, a guard on the team, said that Mears appeared to enjoy getting the Vandy fans' goat.

"When we would show up at the gym," said Justus in an article that appeared in *Nashville Sports Weekly* on February 15, 2000, "the fans reacted as fans will, and it was a tactic on his part to come out in his orange blazer on the floor and walk all the way to the dressing room. Instead of being discreet, he made the walk very slowly. And as he did, the fans reacted to him and it let us get into the dressing room without taking that kind of heat.

"It was a little bit of a psychological ploy on his part. I cannot say that he didn't enjoy it, because I think he did. He didn't announce the walk to us; it just became a thing he did ... After he did it, he used it more and more. In the end, the Vanderbilt crowd didn't know whether to get stone silent or to continue to react to his walk. Either way, it let it be known that he got their attention, which was his whole idea."

Ironically, Vanderbilt's coach at the time was also named Skinner (Roy Skinner) and Mears said that Skinner never liked him. But Skinner at least respected him.

"He added that certain element to the game," Roy Skinner, told the *Tennessean* in Nashville after Mears' death. "I remember him walking around our court with his muscle man. He sure got the crowd excited.

"The fans didn't realize it, but they were playing right into his hands. That was his way of motivating his team—and it worked."

Mears also planned to have a student, who was a Vietnam veteran, wear a Big Orange costume and accompany him on one of his later walks.

"The student went to the fraternity house and made that orange costume, like mascots of today," said Mears in the *Nashville Sports Weekly* article. "He got in it and I brought him over to Vanderbilt where they wouldn't let him go up onto the court. He said, 'Well, I'm going up there anyway.' And some guy said: 'I'll put you in jail (if you do).' I said: 'We're not going to do that.' They wrote to the commissioner's office and told him about the unicycle rider, thinking it was going to cause a riot.

"The commissioner said: 'We can't afford to take a chance on a riot, so you can't use him.' So we never used the unicycle after that. They didn't stop me from walking.

"I knew our rivals were Kentucky and Vanderbilt, so I tried to get our kids stirred up for them. The hatred at Vandy was greater than at Kentucky. They hated us with a passion and I believe they still do. They always hated us and they always will, as far as I can see it."

Mears delighted in fueling that hatred. He also waited until Vanderbilt's players got on the floor and then would have his team take advantage of what was then "visitors' rights" and force the Commodores to move to the other end.

Mears said C.M. Newton, who was head coach at Alabama at the time, tried a similar ploy against him but had it backfire.

"C.M. had an assistant come and tell us which end of the floor he wanted," said Mears. "He asked for the end where we normally warmed up. I didn't say anything to my players and let them warm up there. When C.M. came out, he got mad and said: 'I thought I told you I wanted that end!' I told my players to move to the other end and told them Alabama was 'running us off our end' and that made our players mad. C.M. was trying to gig me, but instead, I got him."

Mears and Newton remained friends and Mears said they would chuckle about the incident when they got together.

The situation at Vanderbilt escalated to where Vandy fans started throwing oranges. Finally, in 1972, SEC Commissioner Coleman asked Mears not to take his walk and that Bill Seale—who had succeeded Peltz on the unicycle—not ride it during his pre-game act. Mears complied.

Guard Billy Hann said that Mears always went out of his way to make sure his team was up for Vanderbilt. In 1970, when Hann was a graduate assistant for Mears, Vanderbilt was paying a return visit to Knoxville after the incident with Skinner and where the students threw oranges at the team.

"This time, they were in Big Orange Country and Ray wanted to make sure that we did more than win and they paid for what they did to us previously. As a graduate assistant, I normally stood at the back of the meeting room. Players were always asked to be seated in the meeting room 15 minutes before coach was scheduled to enter (Vince Lombardi time).

"Coach came out, briefly discussed the assignments, then pulled out a blown-up picture of the team being pelted by oranges at the last game. He gave a short, highly motivational talk about what we needed to do to show Vandy what the Big Orange meant to us, then he picked up a real orange and threw it at (over) the seated players and it smashed against the wall where I normally stood. The players all stood and charged out onto the floor. Vandy paid the price that night."

Coach Mears being carried off court after pulling upset over favored opponent.

Mears stressed the importance of the Vanderbilt rivalry in a *Smokey's Tale* article in 1987.

"They were an instate rival and a very strong one," said Mears in the article, "and an ultra-sensitive one. Our fans wanted to beat them as badly as they wanted to beat Kentucky. They, too, were at the top of the league (Vandy and its F Troop won the SEC title in 1974). We worked hard on trying to beat Vandy."

University of Tennessee Armory-Fieldhouse—Venue that Mears' exciting basketball teams and promotions filled with fans. It was replaced with an enlarged Stokely Athletic Center in 1966.

Chapter 13

Success not Appreciated by All

After sitting out most of the 1962-63 season due to his illness, Mears returned for the 1963-64 season and took his team to a 16-8 record overall and a 9-5 SEC record, good for second place in the league.

Mears' Vols did even better in the 1964-65 season, posting a 20-5 record and again finishing second in the SEC overall, this time with a 12-4 record. That tied a school record for victories in one season. The only other Tennessee basketball team to win 20 games in a season previous to that was the 1947-48 team and it had to win two games in the SEC tournament to get there.

Mears' team posted its record without benefit of an SEC tournament, which ended after the 1951-52 season and wouldn't resume again until after Mears' career at Tennessee had ended.

Mears also produced a pair of All-Americans early in his Tennessee career, Danny Schultz in 1964 and A.W. Davis in 1965.

By now, the fans were filling the 7,500-seat Armory-Fieldhouse on a regular basis, making it necessary to make plans to expand it into what would become the 12,700-seat Stokely Center for the 1966-67 season.

When Mears' team continued its success the next year with records of 18-8 overall and 10-6 in the SEC, the new coach had become a fixture and his success was duly noted.

But not everyone was enamored with Mears or the program.

When Mears' team knocked off "Rupp's Runts," a team that included NBA playing and coaching great Pat Riley, Louie Dampier and well-known TV basketball analyst Larry Conley in the final game played in the Armory-Fieldhouse , the coach was feeling pretty good about himself.

UT Sports Information

Mears takes part in ground-breaking ceremony for Stokely Center in December of 1965. Pictured *left to right* **are UT President Andy Holt, Athletic Director Bob Woodruff, Gov. Frank Clement, Mears and UT Trustee Jerome Taylor.**

So when Mears was asked to meet with Athletic Director Bob Woodruff, he figured he was about to be rewarded for his good work. He figured wrong.

"He called me in and said he was going to have to cut my recruiting budget," said Mears. "He didn't give me a reason. I told him, if he did that, he'd put us in third or fourth place in the league and that if I couldn't get that changed I was going to another college. I had a letter from Missouri in my pocket."

Mears speculated that his basketball program was getting too big and that Woodruff didn't want the basketball program getting more attention than the football program.

Mears took it as a slap in the face, after all he'd accomplished.

"I told Woodruff that I was going to go over his head to President (Edward J.) Boling," said Mears. "I'd pretty much made up my mind that, if President Boling didn't back me, I was going to leave Tennessee."

Mears, however, found Boling receptive.

"When I went to talk with him, he not only assured me that I would have at least as much money to recruit with as I had the previous season, but gave me my first contract," said Mears. "He's the reason I stayed … He was very kind to me. There were two members of the administration who were always nice to me—Dr. Boling and Charles Smith, Boling's vice president who was later chancellor at UT-Martin."

Boling suggested Woodruff was of the old school and that's why he acted as he did.

"We were getting ready to undergo a real change," said Dr. Boling, after his retirement. "Coach Mears was a real change for us. He was the first basketball coach we had who wasn't also a football coach. It was a first not only for us, but one of the first in the conference (other than at Kentucky).

"We were getting ready to upgrade several sports with Chuck Rohe in track and Ray Buzzard in swimming. I didn't know if Woodruff would be good for the job or not because he was purely a football man. But he got Buzzard to coach swimming, even though he was coaching football at Chattanooga. I don't know how he ever became such a good swimming coach, but he did."

In light of the way Boling "saved" Mears and his Tennessee program, it's only fitting that Boling's name is on the current home of the Basketball Vols—Thompson-Boling Arena.

UT Sports Information

Last game to be played in Tennessee's Armory-Fieldhouse. Mears orchestrated a major upset victory over Adolph Rupp's highly-ranked team known as "Rupp's Runts."

Chapter 14

The Star System: All-Americans on Parade

Not only did Mears produce victories early in his career at Tennessee, he produced All-Americans by using his "Star System."

Danny Schultz, the sharp-shooting guard from Hiwassee Junior College, was his first All-American. Schultz averaged 18.3 points per game in 1963-64 to lead the Vols to a second-place SEC finish. A.W. Davis followed him in 1965, leading the team with a 19.6 average and Red Robbins earned the honor in 1966 when he averaged 17.1 points and 12.6 rebounds.

Ron Widby, who may be the only athlete to letter in four different sports at Tennessee during his career—golf and baseball, as well as football and basketball—followed suit in 1967 when the Vols won their first SEC title under Mears. Widby, a Knoxville native, averaged 22.1 points a game and scored a school-record 50 points in one game his senior year to pick up the honor.

Mears' knack of getting the ball to his scorers was so successful that Tom Boerwinkle (1968) and Billy Justus (1969) completed a run of six straight years with an All-American from 1964 through 1969.

Others to make All-American under Mears at Tennessee included Jimmy England (1971), Bernard King (1975-76-77) and Ernie Grunfeld (1976-77).

"I used the Star System throughout my career," said Mears. "I used it everywhere I was—at Wittenberg and at Tennessee, as well as in high school. I wasn't a great basketball player or a mental genius, but what I did do was associate with great coaches. While I was a coach in high school, I got a chance to go to a camp held by the great Clair Bee. He coached Long Island University located in Brooklyn, New York and was the No. 1 coach in America at the time and one of the all-time best. I was only twenty-five-years old at the time. I wanted to be the best by learning from the best.

"A friend from the service had ties that got me to his camp. He brought in all the best coaches; Rupp was among them. Press Maravich was the head of the camp and he put me in charge of tennis. They had other activities besides basketball for the boys in his camp, but he let me off to attend the coaching clinics and I heard from all the great ones.

"I had a session with Bee and he gave me some things, but said I had to develop my own philosophy."

Clair Bee, the all-time winningest coach on a percentage basis, was Mears' idol.

Part of that philosophy was to go with a point guard at a time when most everyone else was imitating Rupp's use of a two-guard backcourt.

"I always thought it was easier to have one guy run the offense and get the ball to the scorers. He can run the club better than two men," said Mears.

Not only did Mears have scorers and a point man, who distributed the ball, but designated rebounders. Each man had a job to do on the floor.

"A lot of the Star System came from my interest in football," said Mears. "The Cleveland Browns had Jim Brown and Marion Motley and those two ran the ball 70 percent of the time. Paul Brown was astute. He took advantage of every opportunity. Bear Bryant was also very good at that and so was Vince Lombardi. They took advantage of their talent.

"Rodney Woods was very good at knowing what I wanted. He averaged 12 points a game, but could have averaged a lot more. Johnny Darden was also a very good point guard. He took no more than five or six shots a game and spent his time getting the ball to King and Grunfeld."

Woods, in fact, averaged 32.0 per game in high school.

"Coach told me when I got to Tennessee, I wouldn't be averaging points like I did in high school," said Woods. "But in my first freshman game, I scored 36."

But when Woods got to the varsity, his role changed and he wound up leading the SEC in assists three straight seasons. He now teaches what was preached to him and turned into one of the top high school coaches in Kentucky.

John Ward said the Star System was one of the keys to Mears' success.

"It was very unusual to have two of the top five players in the country on the same team," said Ward. "But that's what you had in King and Grunfeld. Reggie Johnson was a nice player, Mike Jackson was a nice player and Johnny Darden was the point man, with Rodney Woods the point guard before him. Doug Ashworth started his last year and was a role player.

"Mears said there was only one thing worse than not having a great shooter and that was to have five great shooters. He played a role-type system and the system with his last team was King and Grunfeld were the ones who were going to score."

Each of Mears' Tennessee All-Americans had a special quality.

"Schultz may have been the best shooter we ever had," said Mears. "Vanderbilt had a great one in Clyde Lee, but Danny outplayed him in Nashville. He had something like 35 of our 52 points and we won the game. And as a point man, he was just as good handling the ball as Johnny Darden.

"A.W. was also a great, great shooter and he was 6'7". He could drive off the high post like lightning and he was just a good basketball player as well as being a great shooter. He's one of the best we ever had. I wouldn't put him in a class with King, but he was right up there with Ernie. An interesting thing about A.W. is that his mother and father went everywhere we did and saw all of his games. I don't remember anyone else (parents) doing that.

"We signed Robbins in 1964. He was 6'9" and could shoot with A.W. I played Sid Elliott ahead of him his first year, but the next two he played excellent basketball for us. He went on and played in the ABA for 10 or 12 years."

Widby came to Tennessee on a football scholarship, but didn't really want to play football once he arrived.

"Like most kids in high school, I played all sports," said Widby. "My senior year, I suffered a broken arm and shoulder. I was offered a college football scholarship by Tennessee and accepted it because I always wanted to go there. But I didn't know how my arm and shoulder would heal.

"After healing up 100 percent, I had a good year in basketball and decided I did not want to play football any more. The coaches kept me on football scholarship, hoping I'd change my mind. I did not. Right before freshman football practice started, Coach Mears asked me if I would be interested in punting for the team because they needed a punter. After the season, the football coaches asked me to punt the next season for the varsity. Neither Coach Mears nor I had a problem with this and the rest is history. Coach Mears' unselfishness had helped UT's football program and launched a new career for me."

"He liked basketball and he wasn't going to stay unless they let him play basketball. Bowden Wyatt gave his okay," said Mears. "Had he been on basketball scholarship, he couldn't play football, but by being on football scholarship he could do both. I encouraged him to help the football team out with his punting and that's the best thing that ever happened to him because he was a better football player as a punter than he was a basketball player. He became such a great punter that he still holds a record in Dallas (for longest punt, 84 yards in 1968)."

Widby, who averaged 43.8 yards per punt for Tennessee in 1966 to lead not only the SEC, but the nation, signed as a free agent with the Cowboys in 1968 and played for them through the 1971 season. He also played with the Green Bay Packers from 1972-74. Widby also played a season of pro basketball with the New Orleans Bucs of the ABA in the 1967-68 season. Widby averaged 42.3 yards per punt in his career—third all-time in Tennessee history. He made All-American in both football and basketball his senior season.

Boerwinkle was a project who matured, academically as well as physically.

"In high school, he was 6'10" and skinny; about 210 pounds," said Mears. "Rupp saw him and said he couldn't play a lick. They took him down to Carson-Newman and they wouldn't give him a

UT Sports Information

Ron Widby was the star of the 1967 SEC championship team. Ron was also the star punter on the UT football team. For years, he played for the Dallas Cowboys.

scholarship. But Bill Gibbs came to me and said we had a chance to get a seven-footer. He said he's not very good, but I asked if he wanted him and he did. He was the last kid we signed that year.

"The first year, he was so bad that by the time he got to half court, we'd already scored. Anyone who saw him said he was the worst basketball player they'd ever seen."

Boerwinkle was also unimpressive in the classroom, recording such a poor academic record that he was nearly expelled from school.

But Mears didn't give up.

Academically, Dean of Students Charlie Burchett intervened and Boerwinkle got his grades up enough to play his second season after taking a red-shirt his first year.

"He was very good at teaching kids how to study," said Mears in praise of Burchett.

Meanwhile, there was a concerted effort to help Boerwinkle improve physically.

"Two things happened," said Mears. "First, he didn't have any stamina, so Jimmy Cornwall would take him out and run on his heels. We also got him in a health studio (where he did strength training under John Paschal). We couldn't take him out there, but everyone knew him and he had no problem getting a ride hitchhiking. He improved his weight from 218 pounds to 278 pounds. And Stu Aberdeen got him to where he could do a lot of things under the boards and he could score 10 points a game for us as a junior."

By his senior year, Boerwinkle matured into one of the nation's top big men. He averaged 15.2 points and 11.3 rebounds per game en route to All-American honors in 1968.

"He was our first big man to make All-American," said Mears. "He started for the Bulls for something like 10 years and they nearly won an NBA title with him."

Boerwinkle later won three NBA Championships rings with the Bulls, but as a broadcaster in the Michael Jordan years.

"Of all the great Tennessee players taken in the draft by NBA teams—Bernard King, Ernie Grunfeld, Dale Ellis and Allan Houston—none was taken higher than Tom was," said his teammate on that 1967 SEC champion team Billy Justus in introducing him at the Big Orange Tipoff Club meeting in February of 2007. "He is second all-time in rebounds for the Bulls and seventh in assists. He proved he was not only good enough to play for Kentucky, but for anyone in the nation."

Justus' reference was to a story he told in which Rupp called Mears to tell him about a tall, skinny kid attending a military school near Lexington.

"There's a seven-footer up here you oughta look at," related Justus. "He'll never be good enough to play for me, but he might be able to play for you."

Mears sent an assistant to see him, set up a visit by Boerwinkle to Knoxville and when Tennessee offered a scholarship, the Cleveland, Ohio native accepted.

He would have been considered a project in this day and age and he was certainly that for Mears and Tennessee.

Boerwinkle played freshman ball, then red-shirted. He played sparingly as a sophomore, averaging just 3.6 points and 3.6 rebounds per game.

"I really wasn't ready to play," said Boerwinkle, "until my junior year."

But that is when he started blossoming, averaging a double-double—12.0 points and 10.2 rebounds per game and helped the Vols' "Fearless Five" win the SEC title when they beat Mississippi State in triple overtime in Starkville to win the school's first SEC title in 20 years and qualify for the NCAA tournament.

"That was really big," said Boerwinkle, "because in those days only 16 teams advanced to the NCAA tournament.

Tom Boerwinkle arrived as a project, but left as an All-American.

You had to be the SEC champion to qualify. And by doing that, we denied Kentucky a trip."

The previous year, Kentucky had advanced to the national championship game where it lost to Texas Western—now UTEP.

Tennessee lost to Dayton in a first-round NCAA tournament game in 1967, 53-52, but Boerwinkle said it was memorable just getting there.

The next year, he started to get word that the NBA was interested. He was in the right place at the right time to be picked high by the Bulls.

"The Bulls were a new team. They'd only been in existence a couple years, and they needed a center and someone who could distribute the ball and that was one of my strengths," said Boerwinkle. "Wes Unseld was the No. 1 pick that year and Elvin Hayes was the second pick. I don't remember who was No. 3, but I was No. 4.

"The general manager didn't want to take a chance on me. He said I'd never make it. But Dick Motta wanted me and that's why they took me."

He was also helped by the fact the Denver Nuggets had picked him in the ABA Draft that was held before the NBA Draft and the Bulls were worried about losing him to them.

Boerwinkle went on to play against greats Wilt Chamberlain, Bill Russell and Nate Thurman and also played later against Kareem Abdul Jabbar.

Boerwinkle said he would never have accomplished what he did had it not been for Mears and the way he developed him.

"He gave Stu Abedeen a broom to use against me in practice," said Boerwinkle. "He would hold it crossways to keep me from advancing and then when I'd shoot, he used it to swat the ball away.

"I hated that broom, but I'm glad they did it because they got me ready to play against taller players," said Boerwinkle.

Vol players Howard Bayne, Red Robbins and Bobby Hogsett also played a role in helping Boerwinkle develop.

"Howard was physical and taught me to be physical," said Boerwinkle. "Then Robbins came along and he was skilled and I learned finesse from him. Hogsett maybe never started at UT, but went on to play for the Detroit Pistons. Robbins played in the ABA. Bayne never played in the NBA, but was drafted by the Cleveland Browns (of the NFL).

"I was never going to out-talent anyone. I had to out-strength them, out-muscle them and out-hustle them and all the preparation at UT made me able to do that."

Boerwinkle was joined on that 1967 team by Widby, Justus who played guard along with Billy Hann, and Tommy Hendrix. Bayne, Robbins and Hogsett had graduated the previous year. That team finished 21-5 in regular season and was 15-3 in the SEC.

Justus was called "The Adrenaline Kid."

"Next to King, he was the most intense player I had ever seen," said Mears. "He was an outside shooter, a good, good outside shooter."

Justus started all three seasons, teaming with point guard Hann to lead the Vols to that 1967 SEC title. Justus averaged

UT Sports Information

Red Robbins was an early star for Mears.

11.2 points as a sophomore and led the team in scoring his next two seasons, averaging 18.0 as a junior and 16.3 as a senior en route to All-American honors.

England was Tennessee's all-time best foul shooter, making 88.1 percent for his career. He averaged 17.3 points per game for his career, including 20.4 as a senior.

"He was a different style of player," said Mears. "He was a great offensive player who would shoot a fade-away jumper. He made space for himself and was maybe a better shooter than even Justus."

Then there were King and Grunfeld, who are regarded as one of the greatest tandems ever in college basketball. There will be more on them in Chapter 26.

Left to right; **Justus and Hann before 1968 season.**

The fact Tennessee produced so many All-Americans under Mears was not only a product of his Star System, but of his marketing ability.

"You have to look at how many All-American teams there were in those days," said Ward. "He took anyone who made any team and noted the fact he was an All-American.

He wouldn't necessarily be one of the Top Five players in the country. He marketed his players, just like he marketed his team."

UT Sports Information

Billy Justus (43) put on a show in the NIT against Ohio. He was known as the 'Adrenaline Kid.'

Other stars included, *left to right*; Tom Boerwinkle,
Tom Hendrix, Bill Hann and Bill Justus with Coach Mears in 1968 photograph.

Tennessee has had just five All-Americans since Mears' coaching days and one of them, Reggie Johnson, was recruited by Mears. He was a member of the 1976-77 SEC Championship team that held the record for most wins in a season by a Tennessee team (22) until the 1999-2000 team broke that record (26). Johnson was honored in both 1979 and 1980. Dale Ellis, a Don DeVoe recruit, was Tennessee's next All-American, earning honors in both 1982 and 1983. Allan Houston (1993), Ron Slay (2003) and Chris Lofton (2006, 2007) are the others. Mears had nine in 15 seasons; the program has had just five in the 30 seasons since.

Mike Edwards didn't make All-American, but did win SEC Player of the Year honors in 1972, something that would almost surely equate to being an All-American in this day and age.

Edwards, from Greenfield, Indiana, was one of the most-highly sought players Mears had signed to that point. He was the leading scorer in

**Mears with Jimmy England,
who made All-American in 1971.**

Indiana and one of the few players who ever drew an official visit from then-UCLA coach John Wooden.

"Wooden was from Indiana and had a real feel for Indiana players," said Edwards. "But he didn't make visits to recruits very often and asked me not to say anything about it at that time. He just happened to be in the area for a coaches' convention, so that's why he came to visit me. I got my principal out of bed so he could meet Coach Wooden."

But while UCLA was in the midst of an incredible NCAA Championship run, Edwards selected Tennessee over UCLA, Indiana (coached by Branch McCracken at the time) and Miami of Ohio.

"They all asked me why I wanted to go to Tennessee when they played a slow-down style of offense," said Edwards. "But Coach Mears told me he was getting more talent and that he planned to play a more up-tempo style. I trusted what he told me and I liked the school and that's why I came."

**Mike Edwards was an Indiana 'Player
of the Year' and was courted by UCLA's John Wooden.**

Edwards had been Indiana's leading scorer as a senior, averaging 36.4 points per game, but finished second fiddle in the bidding for Mr. Basketball to Billy Shepherd, who went to Butler.

Edwards averaged 17.0 points per game his sophomore year, 19.4 as a junior when he won SEC Player of the Year honors and led the team to a share of the SEC title, and 15.9 as a senior. He averaged 17.4 points for his career and made All-SEC twice.

Len Kosmalski, a 7-footer from Maple Heights, Ohio, was another player who was a star for Tennessee but just missed out for All-American honors. He made All-SEC three consecutive years—averaging 19.5 points and 8.4 rebounds as a sophomore in 1972, 17.0 points and 6.5 rebounds as a junior in 1973 and 16.3 points and 9.8 rebounds as a senior in 1974. He went on to play pro ball with the Kansas City Kings for three seasons (1974 through 1976).

Another near-miss was Bobby Croft, a 6'10" Canadian from Hamilton, Ontario who started for three seasons—1968 through 1970—and made All-SEC as a senior when he averaged 17.2 points and 9.6 rebounds per game and 15.2 ppg and 8.9 rebounds as a junior.

Another All-SEC player under Mears was Don Johnson, a 6'5" forward from Benson, Illinois, who averaged 18.7 points per game as a senior in 1971.

A player of some note that Mears recruited, but who never played for him, was 6'11" Kevin Nash—a Trenton, Michigan, product who played under Don DeVoe in 1978-

Len Kosmalski.

1980. He had averaged 17 points and 17 rebounds per game in high school and Tennessee beat Ohio State, Michigan State, Cincinnati and Tulane for his services. Nash was a reserve for the Vols but later made a name for himself as one of the country's top professional wrestlers.

UT Sports Information

Bobby Croft, a 6'10" All-SEC player Mears recruited from Canada.

Chapter 15

Very Superstitious

It wasn't something that got much play in the media, but those around him knew Mears was a very superstitious person; maybe even a little clairvoyant.

"Mears was the type of guy that if he went to Lexington and lost, they'd stay in a different hotel the next time," said John Ward. "That's the way he thought.

"They were playing at the Sports Arena in Los Angeles in 1968 and the team bus came up to the arena and, for some reason, the bus could not get to the entrance and we had to walk about 400 yards. Mears had walked in with Billy Hann and talked strategy with him on the way in.

"He won the game (78-68), so come time for the next game and the bus gets within 400 feet of the arena and Mears says: 'Stop the bus!' The players said 'Wait a minute, the gym's over there.' But he got off and walked the 400 yards to the entrance with Billy Hann. Every game the rest of the year, he did that. It got to the point where Hann would say: 'Wait a minute. I was on that side.'

"The players were really committed to him and they knew his idiosyncrasies and his weird thoughts. They played on it. That's the trait Mears had more than anything else—the ability to command loyalty. And it wasn't just from his players, but from other people—people who would do things they knew didn't make sense but because of Mears, they did it."

Rodney Woods said Mears also had a knack for knowing when his team was going to pull the big upset.

"One of the more interesting things that happened in my four years happened in my senior season in February of 1975," said Woods. "We had just lost two or three consecutive games, Bernard King (knee) and I (ankle) had been playing hurt and the team was really struggling. On Tuesday, before we were to play Kentucky at home on Saturday night, coach called Bernard and me in and told us we had the week off to try to heal somewhat, if possible. We would not practice a day, yet start on Saturday night against the nation's No. 2 team (Kentucky ended up losing the National Championship to UCLA that year).

"During those days, Ernie Robertson would film about one-fourth of the games in color and the rest in black and white (due to expense) for coach's TV show. But on Saturday morning, Ernie told me, coach called him about 10 in the morning and said he wanted the entire game filmed in color. We went on to win 103-98 in what many have called the greatest basketball game ever played in Stokely Athletic Center. Ernie told me this had happened only one previous time, when coach wanted the South Carolina game in 1969 filmed in color. Tennessee won and knocked off the nation's No. 1 team in Columbia!

"Ernie would tell these stories, making you feel as though coach knew beforehand what would happen. He had that effect on his players. We just knew, at times, we were going to win."

Mears also had his superstitions when he was at Wittenberg.

The 1962 article that appeared in *Sports Illustrated* noted that Mears lived by his superstitions.

"He never changes his starting lineup when the team is winning; he wears the same mustard-colored blazer at every game and every pre-game meal concludes with the same dessert—a dish of green Jello," the article noted.

Chapter 16

The Fearless Five

Of all the teams in the Mears' Era, this was one of his favorites and also a fan favorite because of its dogged determination to win the SEC title when few gave it a chance.

The year was 1966-67 and Tennessee had lost four of its top six players from the previous season, when the squad topped its season by upsetting No. 1 Kentucky in the final game played in the Armory-Fieldhouse. Gone were Howard Bayne, Larry McIntosh, Red Robbins and Jimmy Cornwall.

On the plus side, Ron Widby—who had led the Vols in scoring the previous season with a 17.3 points per game average—was back and so was Tom Hendrix, the fifth-leading scorer with a 7.6 average.

Mears was more optimistic than some others. He knew he had quality coming up in guards Billy Justus and Billy Hann and felt his big man in the middle, Tom Boerwinkle, was ready to come into his own.

"Hann was a Bob Cousy type passer," said Mears. "He was the smoothest ball-handler we'd ever seen here. I went up to see him in the city championships in Cleveland (Ohio). He had 17 assists in that game and made some of the finest passes I'd ever seen. After the game, he apologized to me because he hadn't scored enough for me. But he was what I was looking for (a role player for his Star System)."

"Billy Justus was also a wonderful player," said Mears. "He could shoot as well as anyone we ever had at Tennessee."

Mears had a knack for looking ahead and something he did when Hann and Justus were freshmen helped prepare them for the roles they'd play as sophomores.

One day, the pair got word they were to practice with the varsity that day, rather than the freshmen.

"Billy Justus and I were pretty confident and feeling really good about being asked to join varsity practice," says Hann. "We thought that was a sign of things to come and how right we were.

"Coach said: 'Varsity in one line and freshmen in the other.' I thought that it was a lay-up drill, since the varsity had the ball and we were in the other line. I happened to be the first in the receiving line and instead of retrieving the made lay-up, I was told to run under the basket and take a charge as Howard Bayne drove to the hoop, made a lay-up and knocked me to the floor. After I did this, Coach said to me and the freshmen: 'Welcome to the SEC and college basketball. Now get off the court and back to freshman practice.' This set the tone for Ray's philosophy: No one will give you anything. You'll have to earn it and it starts right now. No coach out-prepared Ray in my five years at Tennessee."

Mears had his shooter in Justus, a big-time scorer in Widby, his passer in Hann, a big-time rebounder in Boerwinkle and a defensive ace in Hendrix. All the pieces were in place for what happened that season.

"Hendrix had great speed and could cover from corner to corner better than anyone I'd seen," said Mears. "We had to change things after he left because we didn't have anyone else who could do the things he did defensively.

"Boerwinkle had the power and Widby was one of the finest athletes we've ever had at Tennessee. I don't know of anyone else who lettered in four different sports, like he did."

Widby was such a good athlete that when the football team was playing in the Bluebonnet Bowl in 1965 he also played with Mears' basketball team in a basketball tournament in Shreveport, Louisiana.

"He played in a game in Shreveport on Friday night and he and John Ward got on a plane to Houston, changing clothes on the way, and played in the Bluebonnet Bowl the next day in the rain," said Mears. "Then, when the game was over, he got back on the plane with Ward and flew back to Shreveport. He got there just before tipoff, finished as the high scorer of the game and was named the tournament MVP."

The parts were in place and the team was also in a new arena—Stokely Center, which allowed an additional 5,000 fans to attend games. All that was lacking was experience. Good chemistry helped the team overcome that.

Lowell Blanchard, former 'Voice of the Vols,' holding court on the team plane. Howard Bayne is *standing to the left* of Blanchard.

"The Fearless Five was just that," said Hann. "We had a really great group of people that came together as the Big Orange. We all left our personal egos in the locker room and were obsessed to win the SEC with one senior (Widby), two juniors (Boerwinkle and Hendrix) and two unproven sophomores (Hann and Justus). We also had a very good supporting cast and we all knew how to play our role. This was another trademark of Ray's—everyone played their role and the power of teamwork and synergy made us a real winner.

"We were not picked to finish high in the conference, but the experts didn't understand the inner strength of Ray and each of his players."

"No one gave us a chance," echoed Widby. "In fact, the sports writers in the SEC picked us fifth in the conference that year. I'm not sure how Coach Mears felt we would do, but he never let us know he did not have confidence in us. We, as a team, never felt anything but that we would win the SEC that year. I had told Marvin West, a writer for the paper, we would win the SEC that year. That was a good laugh for him."

The Vols christened Stokely Center with a 72-54 victory over Michigan. A win over SW Louisiana and a sweep of Auburn and Clemson in the first Volunteer Classic got the team off to a 4-0 start. But when the team lost back-to-back games in the Sugar Bowl Classic to Bradley and Boston College, the doubters felt they were right after all.

Mears' team, however, pulled an upset of Florida in Gainesville (two days after Tommy Bartlett's Gators had knocked off Kentucky) and Tennessee later beat Kentucky in Lexington in two overtimes to put itself squarely in the SEC title chase.

An upset loss to Alabama in Tuscaloosa late in the season put the Vols in a position where they needed to win out to nail down the SEC title. That meant they had to win their final home game against LSU and beat powerful Mississippi State on the road.

The win over LSU was no problem. It was a cakewalk with the players intentionally feeding a red-hot Widby so he could score a school-record 50 points in an 87-60 Tennessee victory.

"That was not my intention," said Mears. "I never went after records. But when he had 42, the players stopped taking shots and started passing the ball to Ron. We've never had a captain better-liked than he was. Billy Justus just worshipped him and that may have been an inspiration for them. Ronnie was certainly deserving. In a poll of Tennessee fans on who the greatest athletes of all time were at Tennessee, Bernard King came out No. 1 and Widby No. 2."

That set the stage for the final regular-season game at Mississippi State in Starkville. Win and the Vols had the SEC title to themselves. Lose and Florida and Vanderbilt would tie for the title, necessitating a playoff to determine the NCAA representative.

"The Mississippi State game was icing on the cake," said Hann. "No one expected us to win. We had to play at Mississippi State, but we had the will to win."

Remembers Justus: "Again, it was Widby's night. He scored close to 40 points and simply would not let us lose to Mississippi State. There was an overflow crowd in their hut that night and every fan came with those cowbells that have since been outlawed."

"It was really like an SEC Championship Game," said Mears, "and it was a great game. Both teams played excellent basketball. I remember they had a guy named David Williams and every time Widby would make a shot, he would answer."

The game went to overtime tied at 64 and to a second overtime, tied at 66.

For all of Widby's heroics, it came down to Justus, however—twice.

"At the end of overtime No. 2," recalls Justus, "I was fouled and had a chance to give us the lead."

But Justus, a good foul shooter missed both foul shots with four seconds remaining and the game went to a third overtime.

"In the huddle, before the third overtime, every member of the team offered me encouragement," said Justus. "Before we went back out onto the floor, Coach Mears put his arm around my shoulder and said: 'Stay tough!' There was one person at the back of our huddle ... that wasn't a member of the team. D.D. Lewis, Mississippi State's consensus All-American linebacker and Super Bowl winner with the Dallas Cowboys, came down to join at the fringe. D.D. had been a teammate of Widby and I at Fulton High School in Knoxville. I am not sure he was rooting against his school, but it made me feel better when he gave me the clenched fist support sign.

"At the end of the third overtime, Mississippi State fouled me again. With the score tied and seconds left on the clock, Widby gave me the same signal D.D had given me. And then, in one of the all-time loosen-up plays, Tom Hendrix walked over to me and said: 'Boerwinkle and I both have four fouls and we're tired. Don't miss this time!'"

Justus tugged on his socks, as he had a custom of doing, and made both to give Tennessee a 78-76 triple overtime victory and the school its first SEC basketball title in 24 years.

"This game was won by a group of players who loved our state, our school and each other," said Widby, "and the man who bleeds orange—Coach Mears."

**Vols celebrate SEC title in Starkville Holiday Inn lobby
after three-overtime victory over Mississippi State in 1967.**

"While one of the all-time great parties erupted back on Cumberland Avenue on our campus," said Justus, "because of foul weather, the team spent the championship night at the Starkville Holiday Inn. Our celebration consisted of throwing everyone, from Coach Mears and Coach (Stu) Aberdeen to John Ward, in the shower and then retiring to our hotel rooms.

"We were greeted by a large crowd the next day when we arrived at the Knoxville Airport. Front and center were many members of the Football Vols with Dewey Warren (the quarterback known as the Swamp Rat) right up on the tarmac."

"There have been many talented teams at UT, some more physically talented, but none more mentally prepared to win," said Hann, who played that season in a back brace because of a slipped vertebrae. "It was the real definition of what Big Orange means to

Tennessee. When it is said that Ray brought the Big Orange to UT, it should mean more than just the words. It is the state of mind, the will to win against all obstacles. To me, that's what the 'Fearless Five' accomplished."

It should be noted that the "Fearless Five," which got its named from an article by Ben Byrd in the *Knoxville Journal*, also became the first Tennessee basketball team to qualify for the NCAA tournament.

In those days, only the conference champion was invited from the SEC. Tennessee, ranked No. 8 in the nation by the Associated Press, was sent to Evanston, Illinois, for the NCAA tournament. There, it had the misfortune of running into a red-hot Dayton team that included the great Don May. Tennessee had a chance to win it late, but Widby's shot bounced off the rim with seconds remaining and the Flyers advanced with a 53-52 victory.

The luck of the draw had not been a good one for Tennessee. Dayton, though it came into the tournament unranked, went on to play UCLA in the national championship game that year, beating three other teams in addition to Tennessee to get there.

It was to be typical of Mears' draws in NCAA tournament. He had a knack for drawing the toughest opponents and never won a game, though his team was always in the game.

UT coaches who won SEC titles in 1967, *standing*
behind their trophies, *left to right***: Chuck Rohe, track coach;**
Doug Dickey, football coach; and Ray Mears, basketball coach.

Chapter 17

Upset in Columbia

Mears says there were times when he just had a feeling his team would pull off an upset.

One of those times came in 1969 when the Vols were to open the season at No. 1-ranked South Carolina.

"I got feelings about certain games and I had a good feeling about this one," said Mears. "It was the first game of the season and top-ranked teams generally don't play well in their first game. We didn't have a reputation for being a really good team and it wasn't one of my better teams (it finished 16-9). But we had some good players. We had Jimmy England, Bobby Croft and Jim Woodall. Jimmy was a great shooter and so was Don Johnson.

"My point guard from Atlanta was sick, so I had to put Kerry Myers in the starting lineup. It's the only time he started a game, though he'd averaged 29 points a game in high school. He played a solid game for us that day."

Myers, in fact, made the clutch points of the game—both ends of a one-and-one with a minute to play.

Mears said his team got a "nine-to-ten-point lead" in the second half, before South Carolina—with future Georgia Tech coach Bobby Cremins at the point and All-American John Roche their leading scorer—rallied to within a point late in the game.

"We had the ball under our own basket and a one-point lead," said Mears, "and I told Myers to call a timeout, if he couldn't get it in. He did, but the official said it came too late and gave South Carolina the ball with five or six seconds left."

South Carolina got the ball in to Roche, whose shot from long range missed, giving Tennessee the 55-54 upset.

"We deserved to win the game," said Mears, whose team went in as a 24-point underdog. "They played a 2-3 zone against us and our wing players scored against it easily. I thought they'd match up against us man-to-man and take advantage of their size, but they didn't."

Late in the game, Gamecock coach Frank McGuire called his two assistants out on the floor to confer about strategy. Marvin West of the *Knoxville News-Sentinel* picked up on it and later said three South Carolina coaches were no match for one Mears.

"Cremins later told me our team was the best team they'd played against all season," said Mears.

Chapter 18

Frustrating Pistol Pete

Pete Maravich from LSU is the NCAA's all-time leading scorer. But not many of his points came against Mears' Tennessee teams.

Though Maravich averaged 44.2 points per game in his career, Mears' teams at Tennessee consistently frustrated him. He scored 50 or more points 25 times in his career, but never against Tennessee.

Pete Maravich, *center*, with his Dad, Pete Sr. on his *right* and unknown man on the *left*.

The Bengal Tiger legend was lucky if he got half his average against Mears' defense.

"He came as a freshman and missed the front end of a one-and-one and we beat him then," said Mears, "and we won five of the six games against them when he was with the varsity."

Mears came up with a special defense to frustrate the man who finished his career with 3,667 points.

"Ray always wanted to win, but was driven to do it his way," said Hann.

Mears' way was to beat LSU by denying Maravich, while others simply tried to outscore the Tigers, who didn't have many quality players other than Maravich.

"Kentucky could outscore them, Rupp had so much talent," said Mears. "Kentucky would score 70 and Maravich 50. But we had to do something special to keep the ball out of his hands."

That "special" thing was to go with a defense Mears called a "T-and-1."

"Since I was the point guard in our normal 1-3-1 defense and had a lot of creativity offensively," said Hann, "Ray decided that I would guard him and the rest of our defense would be 3-1 and collapse on Pete. The rest is history. We held Pete to 17, 20 and 21 twice. The 17 was the lowest in Pete's career and the Big Orange haunted him throughout his career."

"Billy kept him from getting the ball," explained Mears. "And Billy Justus would double-team him with Billy. We would deny him the ball and make someone else bring it up. Where he was dangerous was when he'd bring the ball up and create. But we made others bring it up and he had so much trouble getting the ball that he'd take some wild shots when he did get it."

Many of the coaches who went against Mears didn't like him and Press Maravich was one of them.

"His dad disliked me, just like Roy Skinner (of Vanderbilt)," said Mears. "Press wanted Pete to get his 44 points so he'd get a big pro contract and he hated that I wouldn't let him do it."

Even after Hann had graduated, Mears continued to use him to haunt Maravich.

Hann stayed on as a graduate assistant following his senior year.

UT Sports Information

Billy Hann talks strategy with Stu Aberdeen. Hann shut down Maravich.

"Coach called me into his office before the LSU game," said Hann, "and told me that he wanted me to join the team to LSU this time. Since I often practiced with the varsity, I thought he wanted me to go for that reason. Instead, he wanted me there to continue to haunt Pete. Coach was always trying to get into the players' and coaches' minds. Anything to gain an edge and get them off their game.

"This time, he had me walk across the court before the game to where LSU came out, stand there with my orange blazer and arms crossed and give a mean stare at Pistol Pete as he came out to warm up. It was Ray's way of reminding him that the Big Orange had his number and to get him to see me and think about how much he hated to play the Big Orange. It was like: "Pete, nothing is coming easy tonight!""

Hann later said that when Maravich came out, he was dribbling the basketball and had a shocked look on his face when he saw Hann. He dribbled on past him, then stopped to look back to see if he was still there.

"Some time after I graduated, I saw Pete in Cleveland when he was playing for the Jazz against the Cavs," said Hann. "I stopped to say hello and wish him well during the game, but he wouldn't even look at me and just kept walking."

Mike Edwards said what fans construed as an act of sportsmanship on Maravich's part after Hann fouled out of his final game in 1969 was not what it appeared to be.

"He went over to say something to Billy on the bench and fans cheered, thinking he was congratulating him," said Edwards. "In fact, he said something to the effect that Hann was a no good SOB and he hoped he never saw him again."

That would help explain the incident in the Cleveland airport.

Chapter 19

Little Big Man

Of all the assistants Mears had on his staff, none was more colorful than Stu Aberdeen.

Aberdeen stood only 5'4", but earned a reputation as one of the nation's top recruiters. It was Aberdeen who recruited and signed Ernie Grunfeld and Bernard King—one of the greatest tandems in college basketball history. He also signed an All-American in Reggie Johnson, who played just one season under Mears.

"The first year we were in Stokely (1966-67), he was up in Nova Scotia," said Mears. "I got a call from him and he told me he coached the Canadian National team and had won a national championship. He also told me he had a player named Bobby Croft, who could play for me."

Croft was 6'9" and was averaging close to 40 points a game in high school. He asked Mears if he was interested.

"I told him I was, but asked him why he called me," said Mears. "It seems he went to Tusculum College, even though he was from New Jersey, and liked Tennessee. And Croft really liked Stu."

Mears arranged a trip to Hamilton, Ontario to watch Croft play.

"He got about 40 points that night," said Mears. "Stu came up and introduced himself to me. He had a party afterwards with a cake that read: 'Bobby Croft: Tennessee's All-American from Canada.' I took scholarship papers with me and signed Croft that night."

As for Aberdeen …

"There was no way I could talk to him about a job because I still had Tommy Bartlett. Stu had done all of those things on his own, hoping I'd hire him," said Mears.

Coach Stu Aberdeen with Coach Mears.

As fate would have it, Florida hired Bartlett shortly after that and Mears brought the Little Big Man—Aberdeen—to Knoxville to be his main assistant in 1967. They were together for 10 years before Aberdeen left to become head coach at Marshall, after Mears' final season in 1977. Aberdeen later died of a heart attack while running on the beach. His wife Lynn still lives in Knoxville, also his children—Linda and Mike. Susan, his daughter, lives in Birmingham, Alabama.

UT Sports Information

Mears and Aberdeen coaching on the sidelines.

UT Sports Information

**Mears and Aberdeen during game timeout. No coaches planned or
worked harder at developing their players and achieving victory than these two.**

Chapter 20

Two Who Got Away

Before there was Ernie & Bernie, there was Spencer Haywood—almost. And along with Ron Widby, there could have been Steve Spurrier.

Haywood, who went on to fame in the NBA, actually signed with Tennessee in 1968. Spurrier never signed with Tennessee, but got his only basketball scholarship offer from Tennessee and Mears and may have considered going to Tennessee had then-football coach Bowden Wyatt been a little more flexible.

Spurrier, of course, went on to win the Heisman Trophy as a quarterback at the University of Florida, where he later coached. He is now head coach at South Carolina after a stint with the Washington Redskins. But he was a Tennessee boy and was a multi-sport star at Johnson City's Science Hill School—just 100 miles east of Knoxville. In 1964, Mears approached Spurrier about a scholarship.

"I spoke at his high school banquet and his family invited me to their home afterwards," recalls Mears. "Steve was a great basketball player, as well as being a football star and was also a very good baseball player. I knew he was too good a football player to come to Tennessee just to play basketball and I asked what it would take for him to sign with Tennessee in football.

"He told me he didn't like Wyatt's wingback offense and that he'd have to change to more of a passing offense before he'd consider coming. So I went back and told Wyatt that and he responded: 'I'm not changing my offense for anyone.' So Spurrier went to Florida, where a Tennessee guy, Ray Graves, was the head coach."

The rest is history. Spurrier has gone on to be a thorn in Tennessee's side, both at Florida and now at South Carolina. Not so coincidentally, Spurrier has been known to play mind games with his opponents much as Mears did with his. Spurrier and Mears remained friends and Mears had an autographed picture of Spurrier hanging on the wall in his "White Room" at his home.

"One reason I like Steve is that he reminds me of me. He's cocky, like I was," said Mears, with a grin.

Mears was so cocky in his time that longtime Associated Press writer Bob Gilbert said: "Mears reminded me of a banty rooster the first time I saw him, the way he would strut up the court and anger the opposing fans."

As for Haywood …

"At the time, they thought he'd be the next Lew Alcindor and he went on to be a very good professional player," said Mears of Haywood.

"Stu went up there to watch a ball game. When he came out, his car was jacked up and the tires were gone. It was a rough neighborhood in that part of Detroit. We actually signed him, but he only made a 12 on his ACT test. We brought him in to try to tutor him, but he didn't pass and went on to junior college. That same year, he made the Olympic team and was its MVP. He went on to junior college after that and played one year at Detroit before going to play in the pros."

Added Mears: "Our team finished second in the SEC that next year and with him, we'd probably won the league title and contended for a national title. He might have been as good a player for us as Ernie and Bernie were, if he had the chance."

Chapter 21

Breaking the Color Barrier

Though Spencer Haywood was, in effect, Tennessee's first black signee, he didn't get into school.

That made Larry Robinson, a 6'5" forward, the first black player at Tennessee when he was signed out of junior college in 1971 to play for Tennessee.

"He wasn't the first black player in the SEC," said Mears. "Perry Wallace of Vanderbilt was. But Robby was the best kid to break the barrier for us. He had a lot of pressure on him and signed with Virginia out of high school. He was good academically, but couldn't get into Virginia and had to go to a junior college. He didn't want to go back to Virginia and signed with us. He was a class guy and never had any problems, that I know of.

"The kids really liked Robby. He was a great leader and was not only the first black to play at Tennessee, but the first black captain."

"He was a great person as well as a fine player," said then-Vol assistant A.W. Davis. "In those days, when you recruited a black player he needed to be

**Larry Robinson broke
the color barrier at Tennessee.**

someone special and Larry was. So was the first black player in the SEC. Vanderbilt signed Perry Wallace and he was a really fine individual. We made a good choice on Larry because he was also a super person."

Robinson's junior year, 1971-72, Tennessee had already assured itself of at least a share of the SEC title and had a game with Kentucky in Knoxville. The Vols had won in Lexington earlier in the season.

With five seconds left, Kentucky led, 67-66, but fouled Tennessee's Mike Edwards, a 90-percent foul shooter.

"I took a timeout to set up the defense," said Mears, "and Mike thought he was going to get two shots. But when we came back after the timeout, the guy changed the call and said it was a one-and-one. That startled Mike. I should have called another timeout to settle Mike down, but I didn't."

Edwards missed the shot, Tennessee lost the game and shared the SEC title, but lost out to Kentucky on the tiebreaker that sent Kentucky and not Tennessee to the NCAA tournament.

"Two guys on the team, Len Kosmalski and Edwards, were upset after the game and said they didn't want to go to the NIT," said Mears. "The kids voted not to go back to the NIT. Dr. Boling was not too happy because the NIT was a big deal back then. That was my mistake. We took the vote under trying circumstances and we should have waited until the next day before voting on it."

Tennessee had been to the NIT in both 1969—winning three of four games and finishing third—and again in 1971, when the Vols beat St. John's, then lost to Duke.

The second black signee for Tennessee was David Moss, a 6'5" all-state player from Ringgold, Georgia, who won the state title in the high jump with a leap of 6'8".

UT Sports Information

**David Moss receives the "Most Courageous"
award from Jimmy England at 1974 banquet.**

UT Sports Information

Coaches show with John Ward, "Voice of the Vols," *left,*
Coach Mears, *middle,* **and Ben Byrd of** *The Knoxville Journal, right.*

Chapter 22

Recruiting Ernie Grunfeld

Of all the players Mears recruited, the highly sought-after Ernie Grunfeld was the most difficult to sign.

"He was the hardest recruit for us, period," said Mears. "Ernie was a very bright boy. He was going to pick the school that would help him get into the pros. Tom Konchalski is the one who put us onto him. Stu knew him because he had coached Acadia University and recruited New York a lot. He had recruited some of Tommy's kids."

"In 1962," said Konchalski, who is still active in Forest Hills, New York, where he produces the *HSBI Report*, "Stu recruited my older brother Steve out of Archbishop Molloy High School in New York City. My brother played at Acadia for four years, winning the CIAU National Championship in 1965 and being MVP of the tournament. When he graduated in 1966 and Aberdeen left Canada for Tennessee, we lost touch."

But in 1971, their paths crossed at Jack Curran's Basketball Camp in Cold Spring, New York, where Aberdeen was a speaker.

"He asked me if I would look at players in the New York City area for him and for Tennessee," said Konchalski. "Being an unregenerate basketball junkie and attending tons of game on my own anyway, I was happy to oblige."

The next spring, Konchalski passed along names of two juniors playing in New York City public schools. One was 6'5" Wes Ramseur of Charles Evans Hughes in Manhattan and the other was 6'4" Ernie Grunfeld of Forest Hills in Queens. Initially, Tennessee recruited Ramseur harder of the two, according to Konchalski. It was when Ramseur stood up Konchalski at a scheduled meeting that Aberdeen chose to focus on Grunfeld, instead.

"Stu Aberdeen in pursuit of a recruit was like a hungry dog on a bone," said Konchalski. "That April of Ernie's senior year (1973), he spent 27 of 30 days in New York City holed up at the City Squire Hotel in Manhattan. I had grown close to Ernie and his warm and wonderful family, attended many of his games and arranged for him to play in post-season tournaments with various friends of mine."

Grunfeld's final schools included Michigan, Syracuse, North Carolina, Kentucky and Tennessee. Grunfeld narrowed it to Syracuse and Tennessee before going with the Vols.

"It's a good thing we signed Ernie," said Mears. "We would have been in trouble if we hadn't because we spent most of our recruiting money going after him. When he narrowed it to us and Syracuse, I thought we'd lost him. But Stu felt all along we could sign him."

The key to signing Grunfeld was that the Vols also agreed to take his teammate, Jerry Finestone.

"We were at the Finestone's house and Ernie was there," said Mears. "I told the Finestones that if Ernie came to Tennessee, their son would get a scholarship, too. The kid wanted to play with Ernie and he wasn't a bad basketball player.

"Mister Finestone said: 'Hey, Ernie. Stu and Coach Mears have been up here too long chasing you around. Why don't you just sign and get it over with.' Ernie said: 'Let's go over to my house and we'll sign the papers.' We took him there and he signed the papers. We signed Finestone, too, but we weren't going to sign him before we signed Ernie."

"He was a great guy, hard working," said Grunfeld years later of Aberdeen. "He was very competitive and very focused, infectious. He was always up and always had a positive attitude. He was always a warm person.

"He came to my school every day after school. It got to the point that I knew which gate he'd be at and I'd go to the other, trying to get away from him a little. Nobody else was like that. I had 200 schools after me and no one was nearly as relentless as Coach Aberdeen. He really made me feel wanted. I think Coach Aberdeen had a lot to do with it (his recruitment) and Coach Mears had a lot to do with it.

"The Big East wasn't in existence then and I wanted to go to a big conference where I could play against the best players. Tennessee had a great program at that time. I felt I could play as a freshman because I was playing against college players while I was still in high school. It just seemed a good fit for me at the time. Michigan was terrific. I visited Kentucky and Syracuse was right up there. But Tennessee, for whatever reason, felt right at the time."

Grunfeld and his family were refugees from Romania. Ernie was eight-years old when the family left Romania, where the Communist government discriminated against them because they were Jewish. Grunfeld learned the game of basketball after arriving in New York City.

Grunfeld, who became known as "Ernie G," would go on to become one of the most-popular players in Tennessee basketball history and was the all-time leading scorer for the Vols until Allan Houston, who had a long-time career with the New York Knicks, passed him in his senior year at Tennessee.

Coach Mears and Ernie Grunfeld discussing game strategy on sidelines.

Grunfeld, ironically, signed Houston to a New York contract as Knicks general manager in 1996. Grunfeld, who was drafted by the Milwaukee Bucks in the first round of the 1977 draft, played for the Kansas City Kings and the Knicks before retiring as a player in 1986 and he came full circle as general manager of the Bucks—where he befriended current Tennessee head coach Bruce Pearl. He left there in 2003 and is now the President of Basketball Operations with the Washington Wizards.

Left to right: **Ernie Grunfeld, Bruce Pearl, Tony Jones, Bernard King and Ken Johnson. This photo was taken February 13, 2007 when Grunfeld returned to Knoxville to help celebrate the retirement of King's jersey—number 53.**

Chapter 23

In Pursuit of Bernard King

Signing Bernard King wasn't nearly as difficult for Mears and Aberdeen as it was to sign Grunfeld.

Konchalski put the Vol staff onto King, much as he had Grunfeld.

"Stu actually went up to look at some guy named Farmer," said Mears, "but Konchalski said he's not the guy you need to be looking at. Bernard King is the one you want."

Konchalski knew King more by reputation than on a personal basis.

"Though I had seen him win the MVP as only a junior in the highly competitive Mosholu-Montefiore Tournament in the Bronx and play for his Fort Hamilton High School team," said Konchalski, "I never spoke with him until he led my friend's New York Gems to the Hoboken Y title in New Jersey in April of 1974."

Konchalski called King "one of the biggest steals in the history of college basketball, due largely to his grades and the fact he only qualified at the last minute. He was hugely under-recruited. His only visits were to Dayton, Arizona State and Tennessee, though he was scheduled to visit Marquette (coached by Al McGuire) at the time he committed to Tennessee."

"When King came to Tennessee for his visit, he had just one request," said Mears.

"He wanted a chance to talk with Ernie Grunfeld because Ernie was from New York, like him," said Mears. "So we had Ernie come in and I left them alone in my office to talk.

"He asked Ernie: 'Do you like it down in Tennessee? Did they do what they said they were going to do for you down here?'

"Ernie said Coach told me they'd do this, this, this and this and everything he promised came true."

Basically, Mears and Aberdeen told Grunfeld they'd make him a star and he wound up leading the team in scoring his first season and made first-team All-SEC.

"They told me the same thing," King told Grunfeld, adding: "I think we'd make a good pair."

"He wanted to know what it was like for a New York City kid to come down there and wanted to know how I got along with other people," said Grunfeld of his conversation with King during his recruiting visit. "I told him everything had worked out great for me and we had a chance to achieve something significant here by playing together and winning a lot of games. I told him, down here sports were very important. In the big city, it's about professional sports. The college game is not that big. But at Tennessee, that was the whole game. I didn't know what a great player he was. I hadn't played against him. He didn't play his junior year, when I was a senior.

"For whatever reason, we hit it off right away—two city guys and we both really liked to win. We complemented each other very well. He was an inside player and I was a perimeter player. We both were extremely competitive. We both played hard and understood the game. Though he scored a lot of points, I think he was still unselfish. If someone had a better shot, he'd give the ball up and he was double-teamed a lot. I loved to play with him because of his energy, intensity and his desire to win. We still keep in touch. As a matter of fact, when we lived in New Jersey, we lived a mile from each other for 16 or 17 years."

"I told Bernard 'we're going to get the ball to you,'" said Mears. "We're going to have a good offense while you're here at Tennessee and this is going to be good for you going into the pros. You'll be well-known."

Chapter 24

Ernie Grunfeld & The Temple Stall

Grunfeld burst onto the Vol scene as a freshman by scoring 28 points in his first game, averaging 17.4 points per game while leading Tennessee to a second-place SEC finish (12-6).

"I remember the first time I saw Ernie it occurred to me he'd have made a great tight end," said Bob Gilbert, a long-time writer for the Associated Press who covered SEC games in the 1960s and worked in public relations for Tennessee in the 1970s. "He had the greatest physique and Ray used him to great advantage. Ernie could just overpower people to the basket. He also had great feet. He'd take one or two steps and be in position to shoot, to block out or rebound."

Grunfeld was a great all-around player. He could score driving to the basket and pop the 20-footer from outside.

Maybe one of his most memorable games, however, was a game in which he didn't score many points. But then nobody did.

Mears had invited Temple to play in the Volunteer Classic. Both won first-round games and they met in the finals in December of 1973.

Temple had beaten Mike Krzyzewski's Army team the night before, while Tennessee had mauled DePaul, 96-61.

"They had a good team and didn't need to do what they did," said Mears. "Later that season, they went to Madison Square Garden and won the Holiday Classic."

What Temple did was go into a stall. The Owls led at halftime, 6-5, but a three-point play by Grunfeld in the second half put Tennessee ahead for good.

Rodney Woods, Tennessee's point guard who was MVP of the tournament, remembers Grunfeld's game-winning play and how it came about.

"One of the officials back then was Burrell Crowell," said Woods. "I had a pretty good relationship with him. He was an official who talked a lot to the players. Early in the game, Ernie went in for a lay-up and Crowell waved the basket off and called him for charging.

"On the way down the court, I looked at him and said: 'Burrell. You blew that call.' He told me: 'I know it, but I'll make up for it.' Then, later in the game, Ernie ran right over the top of a guy and scored. The defender was called for blocking and Ernie made the free throw for a three-point play. On the way back down the court, Crowell looked at me and said: 'Don't say anything.'"

It was the proverbial make-up call. Tennessee went on to win, 11-6.

"We were pretty frustrated how that game went," said Grunfeld. "But it will go down as one of the most memorable games in the last 40 years because of the low score. Temple held the ball and we stayed in a zone and never came out to guard them. I believe I was the high scorer with five or six points.

"I don't know what coach told the other coach, but for players it was very frustrating. We felt it would have been a competitive game, but nothing developed. I got two quick fouls and I was on the bench anyway. Fans started booing and were frustrated by the situation.

"I happened to be good friends with Don Casey (the Temple coach who employed the strategy). He was a terrific guy and we have had some good laughs about that game. He coached the Nets about a year-and-a-half."

"After the game, Coach Mears was so upset at what Temple had done that he got on the PA and apologized to the fans," said Woods. "Then he had us play a 30-minute Orange & White Game so the fans would get their money's worth."

"It happened to be a masterpiece because it's something that will never happen again," said Mears. But he said it was unnecessary. "The night before, they looked great against Army and had used a full-court press. We practiced against a full-court press because that's what we expected them to do to us. But when we had a 3-0 lead, they started to stall. You never go into a stall unless you have the lead.

"I asked Don Casey later why he did it and he said: 'Coach, we were trying to win the game.' I told him he'd never be back. I paid him good money to come down and entertain the fans, not do that stuff."

In the infamous Temple game, Don Casey frustrated Mears because of Mears' philosophy of "Attack, Attack, Always Attack."

Another of Coach Mears' coaching philosophies.

Mears in action—coaching the Vols from the sidelines.

Chapter 25

King of "The Hill"

When Bernard King arrived on "The Hill" at Tennessee, he immediately started turning heads with his play and his work ethic.

"Before practice started," said point guard Rodney Woods, a senior when King arrived, "we played some three-on-three games on some nice outdoor courts. A lot of guys came out and played there. Bernard was dominating everyone and some of the older guys were jealous. One said to me: 'Just wait until practice starts.'

"We got to practice and he dominated there, too. Once again the guy said: 'This is practice. Just wait until we play a game. I don't think he's that good.' But by then, I knew he was something special and told the guy he was for real.

"Then we play Wisconsin-Milwaukee in our opener and he scores 42 points. I turned to the guy who was questioning Bernard's ability and said: 'Do you believe me now?'"

King was 6'7" and quick as a cat and used his quickness to rebound better than any other player on the team. King averaged 13.2 rebounds per game for his career—12.3 per game his first year, 13.0 his second year and 14.3 as a junior.

"He was so quick," said Mears, "that one time Ernie threw him a pass he wasn't expecting and he missed the shot. But he reacted so quickly that he was on the other side of the basket before the defender could get there and put the ball back in the basket and we won the game at Mississippi State."

Mears fondly recalls the first practice. He divided the team, taking the guards and forwards himself and sent the big men to work with Stu Aberdeen.

"A few minutes later, someone taps me on the shoulder," said Mears. "It was Bernard. I said: 'Bernard, what do you want?' He told me: 'Coach, they're not working me hard enough.' I asked him what he proposed they do to work him harder. At the time, Stu had five or six big men and was taking turns with them. Bernard told me: 'There's an open basket there. Give me a basketball and let me work on my own.' I thought he was trying to con me. But I gave him a ball and for 45 minutes, you've never seen anyone work harder than he did, twisting this way and that way and making all sorts of moves. He'd learned it from watching the pros in New York.

"He had moves I had never seen, let alone teach him. Who taught him? He did. You can't say his high school coach taught him. He learned all those moves by watching the pro players play in New York City. He worked on those things every night. After that, I told him: 'Bernard, you do that every night.' King taught himself. Aberdeen and Mears did not teach King one thing. My job was to get him the basketball."

Mears said he's told that story to coaches and they said they'd never had a player tell them they weren't working them hard enough.

"He was a special person," said Mears, despite off-the-court problems King had during his career that will be addressed later.

"In the time I was here, I never heard a teammate say anything negative about him," said A.W. Davis, who only coached King for one season.

Davis was assigned to work with King, but noted with a smile: "Bernard was pretty much going to do what he wanted to do. He had things he wanted to work on and that's all he was going to do."

"King was a charmer," said Davis. "He could walk into this room and charm everyone here, if he wanted to; King also had his shy side, believe it or not."

"Back then, everyone was eating at the training table and on Sundays you had to wear a coat and tie for the noon meal," said Davis. "Coach Mears noticed that Bernard wasn't showing up to eat on Sundays and he asked me to see why.

"I found Bernard and asked him and he told me: 'Coach. I don't have a coat and a tie.' I took mine off, we were about the same size, and I said 'Now you have one. And I'll get you a tie so you can eat.' That was probably an NCAA violation."

Still, Davis thought highly of King who was always one of the hardest workers in practice. "If it was the end of the world and someone had to score to save it, you'd want it to be Bernard," said Davis.

Mears said he knew he had a great one when he saw King play in the Boston Shootout.

"He had 16 rebounds in the championship game and was voted the MVP," said Mears. "He was spectacular."

King averaged 25.8 points a game for his career—the highest in Tennessee history—and did it on a consistent basis. King, whose 59.0 percent shooting average for his career is second only to Dale Ellis' 59.5 percent, averaged 26.4 points per game as a freshman, 25.2 as a sophomore and 25.8 as a junior. Had he not taken hardship and gone to the NBA after his junior year, King would have challenged for all-time scoring honors. He finished with 1,962 points and still ranks sixth all-time behind Houston (2801), Grunfeld (2249), Tony White (2219), Reggie Johnson (2103) and Ellis (2065).

King led the nation in field goal shooting in his freshman year, hitting 62.2 percent of his shots.

"King was the best I've ever seen at the college level," said longtime Voice of the Vols John Ward. "And I think he's the best to ever play in the SEC. In my mind, there's no question about that. He had just everything. Grunfeld was the most popular of all time and was the leading scorer until Houston passed him."

King went on to have a great pro career, playing first with the New Jersey Nets. He later played with the Utah Jazz, the Golden State Warriors, the New York Knicks, the Washington Bullets and finished his career in the 1992-93 season with the team that drafted him out of college, the New Jersey Nets.

King, who finished second to UCLA's Marques Johnson in Player of the Year voting in 1977, also finished second to Larry Bird in a vote for NBA Player of the Year in 1985 when he was playing for the Knicks. Bird, while accepting the award, said it really belonged to King who had scored 32.9 points a game that season to lead the league in scoring.

King made history in 1984 by becoming the first player since 1964 to score at least 50 points in consecutive games. He scored 50 points on 20 for 23 shooting with 10 free throws in a 117-113 Knick's victory over the San Antonio Spurs on Jan. 30, and followed it up with another 50-point performance in another road victory—this time in a 105-98 win over the Dallas Mavericks—on 20 for 28 shooting and 10 free throws.

The next season, on Christmas day, 1984, King scored a career-high 60 points against the New Jersey Nets, becoming just the tenth player in NBA history at that time to score 60 or more points in a single game.

But just as his career was peaking, King suffered a devastating knee injury—a torn anterior cruciate ligament—after he fell awkwardly on his right knee against the then-Kansas City Kings in Kansas City on March 23, 1985. It required major reconstruction, causing King to miss all of the 1985-86 season and denying him his explosiveness to the basket that had made him so great.

King said he wouldn't accept a diagnosis that his career was over after suffering the knee injury.

"I asked doctors' opinions until I found one who told me he could rehabilitate me," said King on a visit to Knoxville in February of 2007. "Then I dedicated myself to doing what was needed to come back."

King did come back and averaged 22.7 points per game during his first six games back. But it was clear that King's explosiveness was diminished, and the Knicks released him at the end of the 1987 season.

However, King had a very successful comeback with the Washington Bullets, improving his scoring average each year with the squad and returning to the All-Star Game one last time in 1991, his final full season in the NBA.

After a year-and-a-half hiatus and a brief 32-game stint with the New Jersey Nets at the end of the '93 season, knee problems forced King into retirement. King retired with 19,665 points in 874 games, for an average of 22.5 points per game during his career. At the time of his retirement, King ranked 16th on the all-time NBA scoring list.

King's No. 53 jersey was retired in a ceremony at Thompson-Boling Arena at the Kentucky game in February of 2007 and hangs in the arena, never again to be worn by a Tennessee player.

UT Sports Information

**Bernard King followed Ernie
Grunfeld to Tennessee from New York City.**

UT Sports Information

Ray Mears, *right,* **and his coaching staff,** *left to right,* **Frank Harrell, Tom Deaton and Cliff Wettig**

Chapter 26

The Ernie & Bernie Show

To have two players on the same team of the caliber of Bernard King and Ernie Grunfeld would be any coach's dream. And it's one that Ray Mears realized during the 1974-75, 75-76 and 76-77 seasons when the pair were one of the most-feared tandems in the history of Division I basketball.

They led Tennessee to a combined 61-20 overall record, a 42-12 SEC mark and an SEC title (1976-77) and were forever immortalized in a *Sports Illustrated* article on Feb. 9, 1976 when they adorned the cover under the heading: "Double Trouble From Tennessee."

"It was an unusual combination that will never happen again," said John Ward. "It was very unusual to have two of the country's top five players on the same team at Tennessee."

But Mears' Star System was the perfect draw for two such talented players to wind up at one school. Had they not both been from New York, the combination may never have happened.

Ironically, though Grunfeld helped recruit King to Tennessee, Mears said Grunfeld didn't socialize with King away from the basketball team and didn't approve of some of his off-the-court activities.

"Bernard and Ernie came from two totally different environments. Their common ground was their love of basketball and their intense desire to be the best. But after Bernard had to go for treatment and played on three different pro teams, he was a changed man," said Mears. "Then he went to New York where he again teamed up with Ernie. Ernie was just another good player and Bernard was their ace. Ernie told me then: 'Coach, you can't believe how much this guy has changed. He's my best friend.' He built a house on the same street. He's been Ernie's best friend ever since that time.

"They did get along on the basketball court (while at Tennessee). On the court, for guys who didn't like each other personally and were probably jealous of each other, too, they played together better than any two good players ... If Ernie would have the ball from 12 feet out and Bernard was breaking across, he'd hit him every time. If it was the reverse, King would hit Ernie. King was a great team player. When he fell backwards and made that shot against Kentucky, do you know who made the next two baskets? They double team Bernard and he passes it to Doug Ashworth (Vol post man) and Ashworth makes the next two buckets and we win by four.

"He was unselfish. Most guys would try to hit it—double team or no double team. He didn't. Ashworth was standing under there wide open."

Mears said he didn't start the title "The Ernie & Bernie Show," but said he thought it was a great label for the pair because they really put on a show.

"I think they may have been the best-scoring tandem ever in college basketball," said Mears.

Actually, they qualify as only one of the best. Their first year together, King scored 26.4 and Grunfeld 23.8 for a combined 50.2; their second year, Grunfeld edged King, 25.3 to 25.2 for a 50.5 average; and their final season, King averaged 25.8 and Grunfeld 22.8 for a 48.6 average. The NCAA record book doesn't list tandem records for a season, but it would be hard for anyone to beat the Furman duo of Frank Selvy (41.7) and Darrell Floyd (24.3) who combined for 66.0 per game in 1954. Selvy scored 100 points and Floyd 25 in a 149-95 victory over Newberry on February 13, 1954. That is listed as the best 1-2 punch in a game in NCAA annals.

Grunfeld scored 43 points against Kentucky on Jan. 10, 1976, while King had a 42-point game against Georgia on Feb. 1, 1975, 41 against Georgia on Feb. 26, 1977, 40 against Vermont on Dec. 30, 1974 and 39 against Army on Dec. 19, 1975.

Perhaps their highest-scoring duo effort came in that Kentucky game in 1976 when King added 24 to go with Grunfeld's 43 and also made one of the most-spectacular shots in Tennessee history, from a near-prone position on the floor.

The 1974-75 team set a school record for scoring average that still stands—86.6 points per game. Mike Jackson added 13.4 points per game that season and was the man

UT Sports Information

King makes a key shot against Kentucky, from a near-prone position on the floor.

Tennessee went to if the opponents successfully shut off King and Grunfeld. The 1975-76 team averaged 82.1 per game and the 1976-77 team 85.7 per game.

King and Grunfeld allowed the Vols to go up-tempo and get away from the deliberate style that Mears' teams played early in his career. The King & Grunfeld teams were among the best-shooting teams in Vol history. The 1976-77 team shot 53.5 percent from the field, the 74-75 team 52.8 percent and the 75-76 team 51.0 percent. Only Dale Ellis' team in 1981-82 shot better than the 1976-77 team, hitting a school-record 54.2 percent.

Kentucky was skeptical of how Tennessee got King into school in 1974 and Mears suspects it was the Wildcats who tried to have King declared ineligible late in the 1974-75 season.

"We got a call when we got to Auburn for a game and were told to hold him out," said Mears. "I think they (Kentucky) got a copy of his transcript while he was being recruited and there were errors in it."

Charles Smith, Dr. Boling's vice president at Tennessee, went up to personally check King's transcript and discovered clerical errors that were corrected. King missed just the one game, a 62-59 loss, that left the Vols in third place in the SEC for that season when the Vols posted a 12-6 SEC record.

King made All-American all three seasons and Grunfeld his last two.

King said he and Grunfeld remain close. "That is the greatest chemistry situation I've ever been part of," said King. "Ernie helped me and I helped him. If he was open, I passed him the ball and if I was open, he passed me the ball. And if Mike Jackson was open, we'd pass it to him." Incredibly, King and Grunfeld were All-Americans together in both 1976 and 1977.

But for all their points and all their awards—King was voted SEC Player of the Year each of his three seasons and Grunfeld shared the honor his last season and was All-SEC each of his four seasons—they never won a post-season game.

Tennessee was upset by VMI in the first round of the NCAA tournament in 1976, 81-75, while playing without King, who had a broken finger on his shooting hand. The Vols also lost to Syracuse in the first round in the 1977 tournament, 93-88 in overtime, in a game in which both King and Grunfeld fouled out in overtime. More on that game is covered in the next chapter.

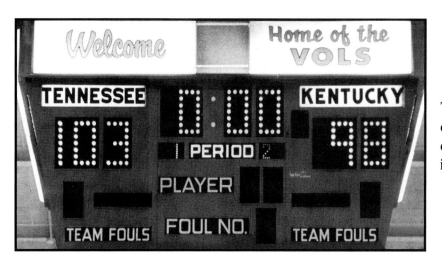

This was the final score of one of the greatest offensive games played in the UT-Kentucky series.

Role players with Ernie and Bernie:
Left to right—Mike Smithson, Austin Clark and Mike Jackson.

Bernard King and Ernie Grunfeld, UT super star players relaxing at Coach Mears' home.

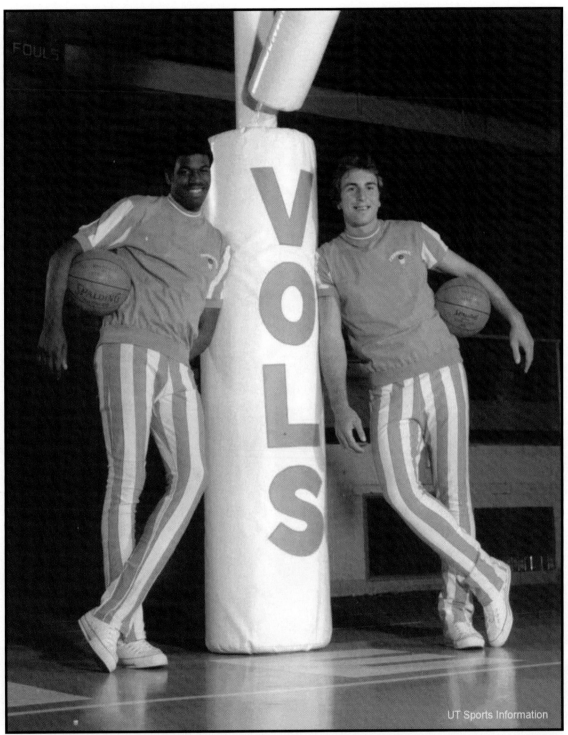

UT Sports Information

Bernard King, *left*, **and Ernie Grunfeld**.

UT Sports Information

Ernie Grunfeld in move against Clemson in 1974.

Grunfeld played on America's 1976 Olympic team.

Coach Ray Mears

*Coach Mears!
Thanks for everything you
have done for me.
It will never be forgotten*

Mike Smithson

**Mike Smithson, one of Coach Mears' players,
became a major league pitcher. He played for the
Texas Rangers, Minnesota Twins and Boston Red Sox.**

Elizabeth Olivier / UTSports.com

The Ernie and Bernie show returned to Knoxville and to cheering Volunteer fans. The occasion was to honor Bernard King and to retire his number. Here two long-time friends and basketball legends in their own right beam, as they are applauded by an appreciative crowd. Appropriately the backdrop for this occasion was the February 13, 2007 Tennessee-Kentucky basketball game and the Vols came away with a four-point victory. Coach Pearl's teams now have a 2-2 record against the Wildcats. After the game, Bernard and Ernie joined the team in the locker room to help celebrate the victory. Ernie spoke to the team saying "Congratulation guys, that was great." Then he joked, "but it's not better than beating them five of six." The Ernie-Bernie duo led Coach Mears' teams that really skinned the Wildcats, winning five out of six contests.

Chapter 27

The TV No-Show

King was selected in the first round of the 1977 NBA draft by the New Jersey Nets, as the No. 7 pick overall.

King declared hardship and not everyone was unhappy to see him leave.

Mears, himself, had mixed feelings but always had a good relationship with King and felt his star got a bad rap on several occasions, including the infamous TV caper.

"Everyone was critical about his off-the-court stuff," said Mears. "But I think they were out looking for him. Every time he was arrested, there was never anyone else with him."

King was picked up by the police in Knoxville three times, all in the off-season.

"His high school coach said we'd never have problems with him during the season, but we might in the off-season," said Mears. "Bernard had a wild streak in him and you couldn't monitor him all the time. The times he was picked up, Stu and I were out recruiting and found out about it when we got back."

Finally, Mears had had enough.

"I told Stu: 'He's embarrassed us enough' and that we needed to do something," said Mears. "So we called Bernard in before the season and moved him out of the athletic dorm into a dorm that didn't have any air conditioning. He wouldn't be able to eat with the other players. We also took away his tutors. This was before his junior year and he needed it for the pros. But if he was going to stay eligible, he'd have to do it on his own. And he did."

Mears said he directed King to a friend, Ralph Allen, for theater classes at the Clarence Brown Theater and King made eight hours of A in the course. King went on to earn several acting roles in major network shows like Miami Vice.

"Ralph said Bernard was well-liked over there. He enjoyed ushering and put on a show. He could put on the dog for you. He thought he was Sidney Poitier," smiled Mears.

The infamous TV incident came after King was drafted by the NBA.

"I have clippings where one guy said they saw the TV in the back seat of his car," said Mears. "Another said he walked out with the TV. But that TV was bolted down on a stand I had and I don't think he could get it off and I remember going down and looking and the TV was still there, but in beat-up condition.

"Cliff Wettig, who took over the team the next season, said the TV was in bad shape and Bernard bought a new TV set and sent it to him. He didn't have to do that."

Mears said King beat up the TV set trying to get it off, but never got it off.

"He had been drinking. But he had already signed a pro contract. He didn't need the money," said Mears. "The thing is, they were going to press charges against him for stealing the TV set. I met with the man in charge of the campus police and (chancellor) Jack Reese and I said: 'Listen men. We've had enough bad publicity out of this. Bernard King has a contract with the New Jersey Nets and we need to let him go and not press charges."

They did let him go.

"I'm told they told him to get out of town and never come back," said Mears, "and he's never been back to campus since."

That was until February 13, 2007 when his number was retired during the Tennessee-Kentucky game.

To this day, King has not been inducted in the Tennessee Sports Hall of Fame and Mears thinks it's for that reason—even though a reader survey in Rocky Top News rated him as Tennessee's No. 1 athlete of all time.

"What he did off the court has a lot to do with him not being in the Hall of Fame," said Mears. "Maybe that's the way it's supposed to be. But I don't think it's supposed to be that way. A lot of other athletes have done a lot worse than Bernard King did."

Mears said that he maintained a good relationship with King and that King's antics had nothing to do with the illness that would soon thereafter force him to give up the job he loved.

"Ernie had a basketball camp in Maryville and he invited Bernard back a couple times to work it with him when both were with the Knicks," said Mears. "A bunch of us went out to eat one night when they were here and Bernard slipped over, tapped me on the butt and said: 'Coach, it was nice playing for you.' I've only seen him a few times since; the last time when he was inducted into the New York Hall of Fame."

Mears was in failing health when King came to have his number retired, but a now-famous picture shows King bending over to greet his coach. The respect was mutual.

**Bernard King greeting Coach Mears
at UT-Kentucky game, February 13, 2007.**

Elizabeth Olivier / UTSports.com

Bernard King leading cheers for an overflow crowd of volunteer fans who came to Thompson-Boling Arena to see Tennessee beat Kentucky and witness the triumphant return of the greatest basketball player to ever wear the "Big Orange."

Elizabeth Olivier / UTSports.com

King is honored at ceremony to retire his jersey. *Left to right* **are Director of UT Athletics, Mike Hamilton, Ernie Grunfeld, King and UT President, Dr. John Petersen.**

Elizabeth Olivier / UTSports.com

**Coach Bruce Pearl telling Coaches Ray Mears and A.W. Davis
that our team will compete with all their might, just as yours did.**

Elizabeth Olivier / UTSports.com

**Ceremony honoring two legends—Coach Mears and "Voice-of-the-Vols" icon John Ward.
Coach Mears is *seated* and *left to right* are Mike Hamilton, UT Director of Athletics; John
Ward and wife Barbara, Dr. John Petersen, UT President; Matt Mears, *standing behind his
father*; Coach Mears' wife, Dana and Coach Mears' son Mike.**

Coach Mears, son Matt and wife Dana watch as a flag in his honor is raised at the Thompson-Boling Arena.

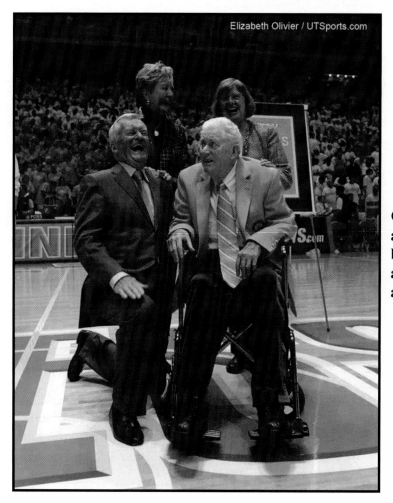

Coach Mears makes a comical remark that breaks up John Ward and their wives Barbara and Dana

As we step back & forth in time, in April of 1981 a roast was held for Mears in Knoxville. A few photographs of this event are shared below.

Announcement of Mears' roast next to floral arrangement.

Charles Smith speaking at roast. Mears considered Charles Smith his savior. He helped resolve questions about Bernard King's transcript and later hired Mears at Martin.

Dr. Andy Holt and John Ward having fun at Coach Mears' roast.

Entertainer Archie Campbell with Ray Mears at roast.

Chapter 28

For The Network's Sake

Something that bothered Mears to his dying day was the pairing made between his 1977 team that included a healthy King and Grunfeld and Syracuse in the first round of the NCAA tournament in Baton Rouge on March 13, 1977.

They were matched in the first round though Tennessee was ranked No. 7 in the nation and Syracuse, coached then by a young Jim Boeheim, was No. 10 in the 32-team tournament. No other Top 10 team was paired with another Top 10 in that year's first round.

"I don't think they did a good job of placing teams in that tournament," said Mears. "We were first in the South and they were first in the East, but we're playing each other in the first round and that's not the way the NCAA tournament is supposed to be structured. I looked it up and (No. 17) Detroit was playing (unranked) Middle Tennessee in the first round. How can Detroit be playing Middle Tennessee and we're playing Syracuse? You answer me that question.

"The reason I don't think (Athletic Director) Bob Woodruff didn't say anything was this was the first year they were televising the games nationally and they wanted good competition and they wanted to be able to sell it and make money. Kentucky came in second to us (actually they were co-champions) and they went some place and had it easy (unranked Princeton in the first round in Philadelphia). Why did Kentucky have an easier first-round game than we did? We beat Kentucky twice. We're the champs. We're first in the South and we play Syracuse.

"I think something's wrong in the way that was selected."

Mears also felt one of the officials who did the game was against his team. It was a Big Ten official that Mears claimed cost Tennessee a game against Marquette several years earlier.

"I saw him out there, same guy, and I knew we were in trouble," said Mears. "I know this guy. He started calling fouls on Bernard and the last one—with about four minutes to go—we go into Bernard and he shot a turn-around jump shot and he calls charging and fouls him out of the game. Is he blind, did he see charging or did he call what he wanted to call? We couldn't do anything about it."

In overtime, Grunfeld also fouled out and Tennessee lost the game, 93-88, and a chance to make an NCAA title run.

"It was a great game," said Grunfeld years later. "You have to give Syracuse a lot of credit. They had a terrific team and a bunch of them went on to become pro players, three-or-four of them.

"In those days, the seeding wasn't done as it is now. To advance, you just had to roll it out there (against whoever they matched you with). We gave Syracuse a pretty good game, but they had a little more than we did."

Grunfeld scored 26 points and King 23. Both also had 12 rebounds in what would be the last game at Tennessee for each. Reggie Johnson also had a double-double with 17 points and 10 rebounds and Mike Jackson scored 12 points. Current Vol color analyst Bert Bertlekamp played in that game as a freshman and scored four points. Johnny Darden had 12 assists.

But Syracuse—which improved to 26-3 with the victory and ended Tennessee's season at 22-6—got 22 points from Larry Kelley, 16 from James Williams, 15 from Marty Byrnes and 12 from Ross Kindel. A couple of future pros, Dale Shackleford and Louis Orr, each had 9 rebounds and Byrnes 11.

Just as it was King and Grunfeld's last game, it also proved to be Mears' final game as the Tennessee head coach.

Johnny Darden was a great playmaker and assist man.

Chapter 29

The Relapse

Mears started having problems even before his final season and underwent shock therapy in Radford, Virginia, as he had in 1962. He checked himself into the hospital.

"I thought it would work and I'd have another 15 years without any problems," said Mears, who had Aberdeen coach the team while missing early games. He returned in time for a trip to Madrid, Spain in late December.

But this time, the shock treatments didn't do the job—at least, not totally.

"I started to really have problems during the UCLA game in Atlanta," said Mears. "It was a big game, on national television and before 17,000 fans and they'd asked me to speak the night before. I started feeling faint again, just like I had in 1962. I told Dana (his wife) to stay down at the reception but that I didn't feel good and was going to bed. Mentally, I didn't feel good and wanted to sleep all the time."

The coach held out until after the season was over, with no one the wiser.

After the season, he went back to the doctor who diagnosed him with a chemical imbalance.

The problem lingered and when the next season neared, Mears felt unable to coach the team and turned the squad over to his new head assistant—Cliff Wettig, whose daughter Patricia Wettig would later co-star on the hit television series *Thirty Something*. Aberdeen had left Tennessee for the head basketball coaching job at Marshall.

With Mears and Aberdeen both gone from the sidelines and Ernie, Bernie and Mike Jackson gone, the team slumped to an 11-16 record.

The veteran coach made a proposal to Woodruff near the end of the season that he have two coaches run the team on the floor and let him overlook the program—much as Phil Jackson later did with the Chicago Bulls.

But Woodruff, who still apparently hadn't forgiven him for going over his head to Dr. Boling in 1966, denied his request. With Mears not even aware it was going to happen, Woodruff issued a release at the Auburn game in Alabama that Mears had resigned.

"He typed up the release before anything was ever said to me," said Mears. "They released it to the press down there. They never called a press conference in Knoxville and the press release was an unpleasant surprise to me."

Ironically, on the last night of the season in tiny Auburn, Alabama, the team finally got the word on Mears. He was finished. Mears got the word from Woodruff earlier in the afternoon that he wouldn't accept Mears' plan to have others coach on the floor and let him supervise the program from a distance. That being the case, Mears said he would step aside and let someone else run the program. Mears thought it would be settled back in Knoxville, but Woodruff made the announcement after the game in Auburn.

The one-page release issued to the press on March 6, 1978 read as follows:

"All of us who love Tennessee athletics regret very much that Coach Ray Mears had decided not to return next year as Tennessee basketball coach," said Woodruff in the press release. "He is a great coach, and the Mears Era has provided Tennessee with an excellent basketball program and record. I hope that he will remain at Tennessee in some other capacity, and he certainly will be afforded this opportunity.

"I am making this announcement immediately after the last game of the season so that we can initiate a search for the best basketball coach available. Certainly, consideration will be give to Coach Wettig and his staff, who have performed admirably under adverse conditions, along with other coaches elsewhere who are interested in continuing the fine tradition of Tennessee basketball.

"I hope to begin interviews as soon as possible and to have a recommendation for the Executive Committee of the Athletics Board soon after the NCAA tournament.

"In the meantime, I have asked Coach Mears and his staff to carry on our recruiting program in basketball until such time as a new coach is appointed."

With that, one of the most spectacular careers in the history of college basketball was over. The announcement came without fanfare and marching bands, the way Mears did things during his 15-year career at Tennessee ... Instead, it came in a simple five-paragraph press release on black-and-white mimeographed paper. There was no mention of his record at Tennessee, nor the championships he'd won. Nor did it mention his standing among his peers nationally. He was the winningest active coach in the nation following the 1976-77 season.

Mears said Woodruff had tried to frustrate him at every turn, going so far as to take Aberdeen's credit cards from him before he was to make a recruiting trip to New York to see Grunfeld. Mears had to come up with some money otherwise to finance Aberdeen's trip. Woodruff also denied Mears an on-campus basketball camp like opposing SEC schools had.

"I told him I needed it as a recruiting tool, that Kentucky and some of the other schools in the SEC were doing it," said Mears. "He told me I just wanted to make more money with it and denied me. Then, when they hired Don DeVoe, the first thing they did was allow him to have a basketball camp (on campus)."

Mears went off campus with a camp at Knox Webb that he ran for his last 10 years, but it was not lucrative.

Mears, who made $50,000 as head coach, was made a special assistant to Woodruff at a reduced salary of $25,000.

Mears also hired Marty Morris as a special assistant back in 1971 and had him do a fancy brochure that would help in recruiting.

"I coordinated my efforts with the U.T. Sports Information staff and the U.T. Publication Services Bureau," said Morris. "The result was a 32-page publication— *A Splendiferous Decade of Big Orange Basketball 1962-1972*. This presentation of Tennessee accomplishments was received enthusiastically by potential recruits and other coaches extended complimentary remarks.

"Unfortunately, I did not realize that I also would be responsible for selling the publication. George Woodruff, Director of Athletics, summoned me to his office and stated that I would have to sell copies in order to pay for the cost of this publication. Therefore, at each home game during the season, I coordinated sales with the Volettes, female students from ROTC who assisted at home games. The revenue was submitted to the Office of Athletics Business Manager, and eventually all the publications were sold."

Mears denies that King had anything to do with his problems in 1977.

"Everybody says Bernard caused my problem, but if I had all kinds of problems with this guy and he didn't play basketball and we didn't get a chance to play in big games because he was causing trouble, I might have had a problem," said Mears. "But he performed like a gem. He used to get on guys if they didn't work hard enough. I had no problem with Bernard King. Fact is, I loved him to be on my team for what he could do and the way he conducted himself (in season). The football program has them, too, and most of those were in the off season. Some of what they've done is worse than anything Bernard did. What's the big deal?

"I had a problem when I first came here. How's Bernard going to cause manic depression? It's a chemical imbalance. The first thing they said was that they had to find the right kind of drug to get it straightened out."

It took 11 more years for that to happen.

Chapter 30

The Martin Miracle

Despite a career record of 399-135 that included a 278-112 record at Tennessee, Mears' coaching career was over. Mears' winning percentage of 74.7 percent still ranks among the top 20 all-time NCAA coaching records for those with a minimum of 10 seasons.

Mears stayed in his job at Tennessee as assistant to Woodruff until accepting the post of athletic director at Tennessee Martin in March of 1980.

Charles Smith, who was Dr. Boling's vice president, was named chancellor at UT-Martin and is the man who hired Mears.

"Charles Smith was very loyal to me and I try to be loyal to him," said Mears. "He was the chancellor at Martin, which is equivalent to being the president here. He resigned and invited me to his retirement party and told everyone there I had more to do with him getting where he was than anyone else sitting in the room."

Mears was the AD at Martin for nine years. Martin had done little athletically to that time.

"They had been a member of this league for seven years and they hadn't won a championship in anything in that time," said Mears of the Gulf South Conference that included such powerhouses as North Alabama, Troy State and Valdosta State.

With Mears at the school, UT-Martin won a Gulf South football championship, two basketball championships and two seconds, and six straight tennis titles. Mears hired a man who had been in Vietnam and developed a rifle program that ranked as high as No. 7 in the nation among Division I schools at one time.

"I had a knack for finding players and also found coaches who could recruit good players," said Mears. "Our tennis coach went to Europe and Argentina and had kids from all over the world. No one else had ever done anything like that before. They didn't know what it took to go big time.

"I brought Art Tolas in as a basketball coach because he was Dale Brown's No. 1 assistant and I knew how great a recruiter he was," said Mears.

Mears later had to dismiss Tolas because of a controversy over academics and made Tolas' assistant, Tom Hancock, the head coach and Hancock proceeded to win two championships and had two second-place finishes.

In all, UT-Martin teams—after failing to win a single conference title before Mears came—claimed 18 Gulf South Conference titles in the nine years he was on the job.

A mark of Mears' marketing expertise was the radio network he set up for UT-Martin in the early 1980s.

He got help from Bob Gilbert, the Associated Press reporter during Mears' years at Tennessee, who had left that job to work in the Tennessee public relations department in 1969—a job he held until 1996. Gilbert went on to have his own radio sports talk show.

"I didn't know anything about radio and Bob did," said Mears. "That's why I called him."

"When Mears became the athletic director at Martin, he called me one day and asked me to meet with him," said Gilbert. "He said: 'I want to set up a radio network for UT Martin and you're going to help me do it.' I told him: 'That's impossible. You can't get any listeners.' He said: 'Yes, we can.'

"So I got on a plane and when I got there, he had Lynn Amedee, his football coach who had just come over from Tennessee, and Bob Carroll, who was the former head football coach at Martin, waiting. The four of us started on a trip to 20 radio stations in West Tennessee to talk with them about starting up a Pacers' Network."

Gilbert fondly recalls a humorous story from that trip that showed Mears' magnetism.

"Mears was driving a UT-Martin car and we came to the intersection of two U.S. highways in Dyersburg and one of them has a little rise in it," said Gilbert. "We're inside the corporate limits of Dyersburg and Mears is driving about 60. He hit that bump at the intersection and that car with me, Amedee, Carroll and him, becomes airborne and flies through the intersection and comes down on all fours on the other side. I thought we were dead people.

"About the time we hit, the blue lights came on from behind us and I said: 'Mears, they're going to throw you under the jail!' The cop comes up and peeps in the window and Mears rolled the window down and said: 'Officer, I guess I was going a little fast, wasn't I?'

"The officer said: 'Oh, hi Coach Mears.' Then he told him: 'Would you please keep the car on the ground next time?' He didn't give him a ticket."

Mears managed to establish a 10-radio station network that covered all of West Tennessee.

"He was an idea man," said Gilbert.

Mears retired from UT-Martin in 1989, but remained at the school as AD-Emeritus until moving back to the Knoxville area in 1993. Mears underwent single bypass surgery in Memphis in 1991. He had a stroke in 2000 and spent recovery time in the hospital.

Ray Mears as Athletic Director of the University of Tennessee at Martin remained very active in collegiate sports. This is the Skyhawks' Arena located in the Kathleen and Tom Elam Center.

University of Tennessee at Martin aerial view. Coach Mears served as the Skyhawk's Athletic Director for nine years. Just as he did at Knoxville, Mears organized winning teams and created excitement for his programs.

Chapter 31

The Cure

For more than 26 years, Mears suffered with manic depression, also known as bipolar disorder, even during the good times at Tennessee.

"I didn't have emotional problems," said Mears. "The problem was what they called a chemical imbalance. You get it sometimes when you're 35-to-40-years old and it usually comes from your father's genes," said Mears. "For 10 years, they tried different drugs on me and nothing worked to improve my condition. For seven years at Martin, I had to suffer with depression. It wasn't so bad that I couldn't go to work. But it wasn't fun to go to work. If I didn't have a job that challenged me, it might have been worse, but I enjoyed it so it didn't bother as much as it should."

Finally, in 1988 Dr. Melvin Levitch hospitalized Mears in Memphis for nine days of tests. He tried the drug Lithium, a new miracle drug which was known effective 80 percent of the time for Mears' condition.

The drug worked and Mears walked out of the hospital feeling like he did before he ever got sick. The only side effects were that Mears sometimes would slur his speech.

The sad part is that it took twenty-six years for the doctors to figure out exactly what was wrong with Mears and to find a cure. As a result, Mears suffered many sleepless nights and episodes of mania and depression, going from extreme highs to extreme lows.

Mears retired from UT Martin in 1989, but remained at the school in a lesser capacity until 1993 when he moved back to the Knoxville area and built a home in Tellico Village that had a view of Tellico Lake.

Mears still attended Big Orange sports until the end, enjoying football, baseball and basketball games—both men's and women's. He long admired Lady Vols coach Pat Summitt, who started at Tennessee at the tender age of twenty-two in 1974 when Mears was in his prime.

**Mears and wife Dana at their home on Loudon
Lake. They moved back to the Knoxville area in 1993.**

Son Matt is a veternarian in Kingsport and once saved one of the author's cats, while Steve is in banking in Greeneville and Mike is an engineer in Charlotte.

At the home at Tellico Lake that he shared with Dana, Mears had two rooms that served as museum to his storied career—the Orange Room and the White Room. The home overlooks the lake with a wrap-around deck that affords a panoramic view. He also drove an orange Mercedes-Benz that is labeled "The Wizard of Orange" and had a license plate that reads RAM—for Ramon A. Mears. The car finally blew an engine and had to be retired.

Mears was honored by the City of Knoxville, which named a street for him in 1979. Ray Mears Boulevard runs parallel to Kingston Pike in west Knoxville near West Town Mall, Montvue Center and Downtown West. It runs 3,000 feet in length and reduces the volume of traffic on Kingston Pike by providing an alternate means of access from the many subdivisions and apartment complexes in West Knoxville to the shopping areas.

Ray Mears was at heart a loving family man who strived to keep his family buffered from the ups-and-downs associated with being a high-profile public figure. Some of his family photographs are shared at the beginning of the Photograph Gallery section of this book on page 157.

Chapter 32

All's Well That Ends Well

C oach Mears, at one time feared he would die without his contributions being recognized. But in the end, the man was more than given his due by the University of Tennessee—particularly by athletic director Mike Hamilton and head basketball Coach Bruce Pearl who went out of their way to insure that he had his proper place in Tennessee basketball history.

Coach Mears was recognized by UT fans and again heard the applause he had heard nearly 30 years early. He died knowing his efforts were appreciated.

Coach Mears passed away at a rehab center in West Knoxville on Monday, June 11, 2007 at the age of 80 and a memorial service was held for him on Thursday, June 14, 2007 at West Hills Baptist Church in Knoxville. Mears was then laid to rest on Friday, June 15, 2007 with military honors at Highland Memorial Cemetery in Knoxville.

One of the big things that came out at that memorial service was how prepared Mears was in life. Mears had planned his own funeral service; not a year or two before when he was in failing health, but 15 years earlier when he was in good health.

He planned the music, the readings, the speakers and even the pallbearers.

"He sent me a letter," said Bill Justus, one of his star guards when his Tennessee basketball team won the SEC title in 1967, "and told me he picked me because he said I would do a good job.

"He told me in the letter: 'I want you to deliver a message for me. Tell every player who played for me that he was special.' Message delivered and received."

Justus said preparation was the name of the game with Mears.

Mears planned ahead. He even planned the details of his own funeral.

"We missed more dinner bells at Gibbs Hall than we made because we were preparing for games. He was meticulous. We appreciate Dana, Mike, Steve and Matt and the family for sharing him with us because we saw him a lot more in those days than you did. And there were a lot of times we'd gladly given him back to you," said Justus with a chuckle.

Jerre Haskew, who was asked 15 years before Mears' death to be a pallbearer, said that he panicked when he received the letter in 1992.

"Ray sent me a letter simultaneously to the one he sent Billy asking me to be a pallbearer. I was VERY afraid he might be suicidal," said Haskew, a longtime friend of Mears who did a sports talk show for years in Chattanooga and had Mears on as a frequent guest, "so I immediately called him. He said something to the effect that, 'Jerre, I'm doing just fine. Don't you worry. You know me about as well as anybody, and I just wanted to plan all this for the future in case I had an accident or something. I plan everything ahead, and you should know that. It was one of the first lessons I taught you in our many sessions together over all these years about leadership and management.

You have followed and executed them well, and I am so very proud of you. You were the first one there for me when I came to UT, and you've always had my back.'"

Billy Hann, Tennessee's point guard in an era when most teams played a two-guard front, was another of the chosen. He was also asked to deliver a message.

Billy recalled that before every game, Coach handed him a 3X5 card with the first five plays written on it. Billy imagined that Coach might have given him the following "game" instructions.

"First, tell Dana I love her for all she has done for me and our family," said Hann.

"Next, tell Mike, Steve, Matt and their families that I love them.

"Tell my players to get ready for the *Big Game*.

"Tell everyone that I gave my all for the Big Orange.

"And lastly, tell Coach Pearl to beat Kentucky."

Dr. Marvin Cameron, pastor of First Baptist Church in Kingsport, was one of those asked to speak. Mears' son, Matt who is a veterinarian in Kingsport, attends First Baptist.

Dr. Cameron got to know Mears in his final years and recalled some special moments when he saw Mears the happiest.

"When Kevin O'Neill was head coach at Tennessee, I was invited to go on a trip to Kentucky with the team and I remember them saying Coach Mears was going to be recognized in Rupp Arena. I didn't know what the response would be, but when they introduced him, slowly and steadily 23,000 people rose and gave Ray Mears, their long-standing adversary, a standing ovation. (Mears had a 15-15 record against Kentucky while UT's coach).

"On the bus on the way home, I asked Coach Mears how did that feel. He looked at me with a tear in his eye and said: 'I can't believe they did that for me.'

"The second moment I saw him overjoyed was right back there 10 years ago in this very room. The occasion was a memorial service for Billy Justus' father. Coach Mears was here because the Justus family had been important to him for a long time. Almost every player Billy played with was here that night. They all gathered back near that door. (Tom) Boerwinkle towered over the rest. But all of them were giants and Coach Mears relished every moment with them and every embrace. His face was as bright as his orange coat.

"The third was in Greeneville just a couple years ago. Tennessee had a new basketball coach, a fellow who reminded some of Mears. A guy named Pearl. Coach Pearl came to Greeneville to speak to a fundraiser that Steve (Mears) had arranged. He came over to Coach Mears and embraced him. Coach Pearl then began to speak a few moments later and said: 'I want people to hate us like they hated Tennessee when Coach Mears was the head coach. I want them to boo when we walk in.' Coach Pearl went on to describe the traditions Coach Mears put in place and he, Coach Mears, like so many Tennessee fans, began feeling excitement about basketball. For one person named Mears, it was a continuation of a tradition that began so many years ago in an arena that didn't seat 24,000, but only 6,000 if you could squeeze everybody in.

"Coach Mears epitomized so much of his generation. From working in steel mills to being a veteran, to working with legends, his values never changed. Hard work was the name of the game for Mears, whether that was recruiting players or recruiting fans. He believed in character, strength and integrity. He believed in the value and worth of every person. He knew the values of a generation that conquered a world."

Concluded Dr. Cameron: "Thanks be to God for allowing all of us to know, respect and admire this very professional man who created his own country colored with orange—**Ray Mears**. May his memory live on in each of our lives as one who lived an impossible dream."

Post Script

While Coach Mears has received the recognition he so richly deserved from the University of Tennessee, there are a couple more honors that should still come his way.

Though Mears has a room in Thompson-Boling Arena named for him, that includes pictures of the greatest basketball players (men's and women's in Tennessee history) and was also given the Naismith Award in 1963, the NABC Hillyard Award in 1996 and has been inducted into six Hall of Fames—Miami University's, the Tennessee Sports Hall of Fame, the Wittenberg Hall of Fame, the UT Martin Hall of Fame, the Ohio High School Hall of Fame and the Knoxville Hall of Fame, Mears is not yet in the Basketball Hall of Fame in Springfield, Massachusetts. He was once nominated for this honor by former player Eldon Miller.

There is also a push to have his name added to either Thompson-Boling Arena or the new men's basketball practice facility that is being completed.

That effort is promoted by the following poem written by long-time friend and booster Jerre Haskew of Chattanooga.

THE REAL BIG ORANGE
(TO MY FRIEND AND MENTOR, COACH RAY MEARS)

BY JERRE R HASKEW
@Copyright January, 2007

HE WAS ONLY THIRTY-FIVE YEARS OLD
WHEN BOWDEN BROUGHT HIM TO THE FOLD
WITH STU AND TOMMY BY HIS SIDE
HE FILLED US ALL WITH WINNING PRIDE
AND THE COLOR HE WORE WAS ORANGE
HOW WE REMEMBER.....
THE GIANT "T," THE DIMMING LIGHTS
THE PACKED HOUSE ROARED AND ROCKED THE NIGHTS
AT STOKELY, HOW HE MADE IT FUN
THE BARNUM'S MAGIC HAD BEGUN
AND THE COATS THEY WORE WERE ORANGE
YES, WE REMEMBER....

BIG ORANGE COUNTRY ON THE SIGNS
AND BILLY IN STARKVILLE ON THE LINE
A.W, RON AND STOKELY CHEERS
FOR ERNIE G. AND THE KING OF THE VOLUNTEERS
HIS WARRIORS OF THE ORANGE
COACH, WE REMEMBER....

HE DUELED THE BARON; THE ROOF WE RAISED
AND SKINNED THE 'CATS IN THOSE GREAT DAYS
JOHN'S VOICE SENT SIGNALS THROUGH THE SKY
AND "BOTTOM!!" BECAME OUR BATTLE CRY
THE PROUD CHAMPIONS OF THE ORANGE
RAY, WE REMEMBER....

TRAGIC ILLNESS STRUCK HIM IN HIS PRIME
HAD TO LEAVE HIS POST LONG BEFORE HIS TIME
BUT THE LEGEND STILL LIVES ON TODAY
TRUE TO HIS WORD HE CAME HOME TO STAY
WE STILL REMEMBER....

MIKE AND JOHN HAVE HEEDED TO OUR CALL
AND NOMINATED HIM FOR THE HALL
TO HONOR HIM WITH DESERVED FAME
LIKE THE HOME THAT NOW SHOULD BEAR HIS NAME
AND OVERFLOWS AGAIN WITH ORANGE
GREAT ONES REMEMBER....

THINGS HAVEN'T BEEN THE SAME SINCE HIS DAY
BUT FAR BETTER TIMES ARE HERE TO STAY
TO RELIVE THOSE GLORY DAYS AGAIN
HE'S GLADLY LENT A FATHER'S HAND
TO THE NEW ONE WHO LEADS THE ORANGE
COACH PEARL REMEMBERS ...

BIG ORANGE IT WAS MEARS' CREATION
"DOUBLE TROUBLE" TOOK IT 'CROSS THE NATION
THE WIZARD OF ORANGE HAS NEVER STOPPED
WE CLIMBED WITH HIM TO ROCKY TOP
AND HE STILL BLEEDS BIG ORANGE
MIKE HAMILTON REMEMBERS....

IT'S TIME FOR US TO HEED THIS CALL
TRUE VOLUNTEERS, HE NEEDS US ALL
TO TELL OUR NEW LEADER WHO NOW SERVES
PLEASE GIVE COACH MEARS WHAT HE DESERVES
FOR BRINGING US THE ORANGE

HIS LEGACY IS OUR BIG ORANGE HOME
AND TO ADD HIS NAME THE TIME HAS COME
TO ADD HIS NAME THE TIME HAS COME
TO THOMPSON-BOLING AND THE SUMMITT COURT

BIG ORANGE FAITHFUL GIVE YOUR SUPPORT
FOR HIM—THE REAL BIG ORANGE
LET US ALL STAND AND REMEMBER....

HE WAS ONLY THIRTY-FIVE YEARS OLD
WHEN BOWDEN BROUGHT HIM TO THE FOLD
THOUGH HIS GLORY YEARS HAVE COME AND GONE
STILL HIS LEGACY LIVES ON AND ON
IN OUR COUNTRY HE NAMED BIG ORANGE
PLEASE HONOR HIM, REMEMBER....

Mears' Legends Wall. With Adolph Rupp, *upper left*; **with Bobby Knight,** *upper right*; **Ara Parsheghian,** *lower left* **and with Clair Bee,** *lower right*. **These photos are on wall in Mears' "White Room."**

Coach Mears offered Steve Spurrier a basketball scholarship, but Spurrier went to Florida and won a Heisman Trophy in football. Mears, early-on, felt Spurrier would become a sports legend.

Mears' orange Mercedes—Legend.

MORE PHOTOGRAPHS...

Photographs can personalize history and evoke memories in ways that words can't match. More than 130 photographs are used throughout this book to help personalize Mears' journey that led him to the University of Tennessee and evoke memories of his commitment and contributions to his players, the University of Tennessee and his/our "Big Orange Country." Most of the photographs have been integrated into the flow of the text. But, so many great photographs were available from Mears' own collection and University of Tennessee archives that we have included more in this section. In a few cases, we have repeated photos used in the text, so they could be presented in color.

Photo by Donnell Field

**Mears at entrance to his
Big Orange Room.**

Photo by Donnell Field

**Mears' top players were
"Double Trouble," Ernie Grunfeld and Bernard King.**

157

The Ray Mears Family,
left to right: Mike, Dana,
Matt, Ray and Steve

Ray Mears with sons, *left to right*, Mike and Steve.

Ray Mears and wife Dana at football party during his final year of coaching.

UT Sports Information

Ray Mears Family, *left to right*, **Steve; Matt, sitting; Ray; wife Dana and Mike.**

A street in West Knoxville was named for Mears.

This is a rug Mears had made to commemorate his biggest win over Rupp.

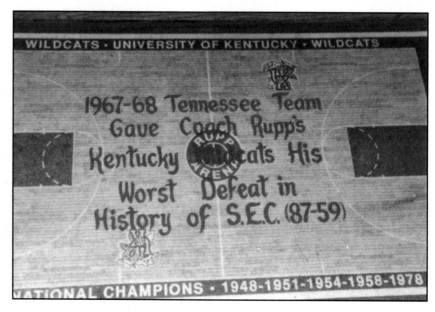

The Mears Family backstage at the Grand Ole Opry.
Left to right: **Dana Mears, Roy Acuff, Matt Mears** *(in front)***, Mike Mears, Steve Mears, Coach Mears, Huell Howser and Bashful Brother Oswald.**

This bedspread was made when Mears was the nation's winningest coach following retirements of John Wooden and Adolph Rupp in 1976.

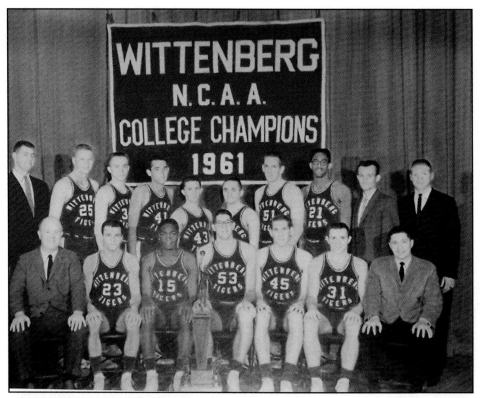

Ray Mears with his 1961 Wittenberg National Championship Team

Big Orange Country was on more than billboards.

Mears with his Orange Mercedes.

Ray playing with Mr. Orange, a Bengal cat.

Mears at home.

Long-time rivals and friends Ray Mears, wearing his orange jacket, and Adolph Rupp, wearing his classic brown suit.

Interior view of the Armory-Fieldhouse. Only 400 fans saw the last UT game before Mears' arrival. Mears' teams and promotions soon had the seats filled with cheering fans.

Vols celebrate triple-overtime victory in Starkville, MS in 1967.

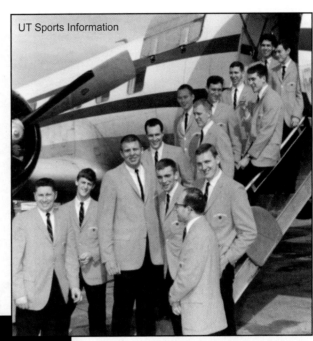

Mears and his players getting off plane wearing their orange jackets.

Left to right: John Petersen, John Ward and Ray Mears

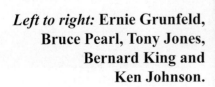

Left to right: Ernie Grunfeld, Bruce Pearl, Tony Jones, Bernard King and Ken Johnson.

Billy Justus and Ray Mears, 1981

**Ernie Grunfeld speaking at the
Mears' Roast in 1981**

**Coach Bruce Pearl resurrects the Big Orange
traditions by wearing an orange blazer at
the Vanderbilt and Kentucky games.**

Mears speaking at his 1981 Roast.

Photo by Ron Bliss

Photo by Ron Bliss

Above: **Some of the Big Orange Tip-Off Club members with Tom Boerwinkle.**
Left to right: **Mark Hancock, R. Larry Smith, Charlie Morgan, Tom Boerwinkle, Lloyd Richardson, Christie Gentry and Barry Smith.**

Left: **Tom Boerwinkle makes a point to Coach Bruce Pearl and fomer teammate Billy Justus**

Tom Boerwinkle displaying his three Chicago Bull NBA championship rings.

Photo by Ron Bliss

During his basketball coaching career, Ray Mears accumulated some amazing winning statistics. The following appendices detail his records and documents the players and coaches associated with him throughout his coaching career.

Mears' career winning percentage record was .747. A Boeing 747 model plane, built by one of his sons, and kept in his den displays this information.

Appendices

Ray Mears' Season-By-Season Collegiate Records

At Wittenberg College:

Season	Record	Winning Percent	Notes
1956-57	15-7	.714	First winning season since '52-53
1957-58	19-3	.864	Best single-season in history
1958-59	19-3	.864	First OAC title since '45-46
1959-60	22-2	.917	OAC titles, NCAA Regional
1960-61	25-4	.862	OAC and NCAA National Champs
1961-62	21-5	.808	OAC Champions, NCAA Regional
Totals	**121-23**	**.840**	

At University of Tennessee:

Season	Record	Winning Percent	Notes
1962-63	13-11	.541	6-8, 7th in SEC
1963-64	16-8	.667	9-5, 2nd in SEC
1964-65	20-5	.800	12-4, 2nd in SEC
1965-66	18-8	.692	10-6, T 3rd in SEC
1966-67	21-7	.750	15-3, SEC champs, NCAAs
1967-68	20-6	.769	13-5, 2nd SEC
1968-69	21-7	.750	13-5, 2nd SEC, 3rd in NIT
1969-70	16-9	.640	10-8, 5th in SEC
1970-71	21-7	.750	13-5, 2nd in SEC, 3rd in NIT
1971-72	19-6	.760	14-4, T 1st in SEC
1972-73	15-9	.625	13-5, T 2nd in SEC
1973-74	17-9	.654	12-6, 2nd in SEC, CCA Bid
1974-75	18-8	.692	12-6, T 3rd in SEC, NCIT Bid
1975-76	21-6	.777	14-4, 2nd in SEC, NCAA regional
1976-77	22-6	.786	16-2, T 1st in SEC, NCAA regional
Totals	**278-112**	**.713**	**182-76 in SEC (.805)**
Career			
*Totals	**399-135**	**.747**	

169

Mears' Career Notes

Coach of Year Awards: 1960 Ohio Coach of the Year; 1967 and 1977 SEC Coach of the Year.

Hall of Fame Awards: Naismith Award 1963; Miami of Ohio Hall 1977; Tennessee Sports Hall 1985; Wittenberg Hall 1987; UT-Martin Hall 1989; Ohio High School Hall 1995; NABC Hillyard Award 1996; Knoxville Hall 1997.

Other Coaching Jobs: Cadiz High School, Cadiz, Ohio 1949-50; West Tech High School, Cleveland, Ohio 1952-56.

Other Awards: Teams led either NCAA Division I or College Division in defense five times; Wittenberg won 40 straight OAC games from 1959 through 1961; team won record 69-straight home games in his career at Wittenberg; coached two All-Americans at Wittenberg and nine more at Tennessee; players made first-team All-Conference eight times at Wittenberg and 27 times at Tennessee.

Wittenberg College Facts

NCAA Playoff Games Under Ray Mears

1959 Mideast Regional
at Evansville, Ind.

Southern Illinois, W, 80-70
Evansville, Ind., L, 56-50

1961 Mideast Regional
at Crawfordsville, Ind.

Youngstown, W, 43-28
Wabash, Ind., W, 48-42

1961 NCAA Championships
at Evansville, Ind.

Williams, Mass., W, 64-51
Mount St. Mary's, Md., W, 65-49
Southeast Missouri, W, 42-38
(National Champions)

1962 Mideast Regional
at Akron, Ohio

Gannon, Pa., W, 69-43
Florida A&M, W, 35-33
Mount St. Mary's, Md., L, 43-39

Wittenberg College Facts (continued)
All-Conference Players Under Ray Mears

1959-60	1960-61	1961-62
First Team	First Team	First Team
Bert Price, F	Bert Price, F	Al Thrasher, F
Tony Wilcox, C	Second Team	Second Team
Tony Vedova, G	Don Wolfe	Bill Fisher, G

Conference Players of the Year Under Ray Mears

Terry Deems, 1957-58, 1958-59
Bert Price, 1959-60

All-Americans Under Ray Mears

Third Team
Terry Deems, F, 1958-59

First Team
George Fisher, C, 1960-61
Bert Price, F, 1960-61

Wittenberg Lettermen Under Ray Mears

Skender Brane, 1957-58
Bob Cherry, 1961, 62*, 63, 64
Terry Deems, 1956, 57, 58*, 59*
Dave Edwards, 1957
Bill Emshoff, 1960
Ed Erick, 1960
Bill Fisher, 1961, 62, 63, 64*
George Fisher, 1958, 59, 60, 61
Bill Funderberg, Sr., 1958
Claude Graves, 1962, 63, 64, 65*
Bob Hamilton, 1962, 63
Bill Heideloff, 1960
Jerry Hockman, 1959, 60, 61, 62
Marv Hohenberger, 1958
Walt Kindy, 1956, 57*
Bob Lyren, 1962

Steve McCullough, 1962
Eldon Miller, 1958, 59, 60, 61*
Tony Nixon, 1958
Bert Price, 1959, 60, 61
Don Rader, 1958
Roger Rogos, 1960, 61, 62
Don Scott, 1955, 56, 57
Phillip Stanley, 1957
Robert Thomas, 1957
Bernie Thompson, 1957, 58, 59
Al Thrasher, 1961, 62*, 63*, 64*
Tony Vedova, 1957, 58, 59, 60*
Bernie Weiss, 1959
Tony Wilcox, 1957, 58, 59, 60
Don Wolfe, 1958, 59, 60, 61*
*Captain that year

All-Time Winningest Division I Basketball Coaches
(Through the 1999-2000 Basketball Season)
(Minimum 10 years in Division I)

Pos.	Coach	Schools	Years Coached	Record	Win Percentage
1.	Clair Bee	LIU-Brooklyn	1932-45, 1946-51	412-87	.826
2.	Adolph Rupp	Kentucky	1931-1972	876-190	.822
3.	John Wooden	Indiana State	1947-48		
		UCLA	1949-75	664-162	.804
4.	Roy William	Kansas	1989-2003		
		North Carolina	2003-present	524-131	.801
5.	John Kresse	College of Charleston		560-143	.797
6.	Jerry Tarkanian	Long Beach	1969-73		
		UNLV	1974-92		
		Fresno	1996-present	729-201	.784
7.	Francis Smith	Tulsa	1916-17, 1919-22		
		Arkansas	1924-29		
		TCU	1930-34	258-72	.782
8.	Dean Smith	North Carolina	1962-1997	879-254	.776
9.	Jack Ramsay	St. Joseph's	1956-1966	231-7	.765
10.	Frank Kearney	Rhode Island	1921-48	387-117	.768
11.	George Keagan	St. Louis	1916		
		Allegheny	1919		
		Valparaiso	1920-21		
		N.Dame	1924-43	385-117	.767
12.	Vic Bubas	Duke	1960-69	213-67	.761
13.	Harry Fisher	Fordham	1905		
		Columbia	1907-1916		
		St. John's	1910		
		Army	1907, 1922, 1923, 1925	189-60	.759
14.	Mike Krzyzewski	Army	1975-1980		
		Duke	1980-present	771-256	.751
15.	Fred Bennion	Brigham Young	1909-1910		
		Utah	1911-1914		
		Montana State	1915-1919	95-32	.748
16.	Chick Davies	Duquesne	1925-43, 1947-48	314-106	.748
17.	**RAY MEARS**	**Wittenberg**	**1957-62**		
		Tennessee	**1963-77**	**399-135**	**.747**
18.	Ed McNichol	Penn	1921-1930	186-63	.747
19.	Rick Majerus	Marquette	1984-86		
		Ball State	1988-89		
		Utah	1990-2004	422-147	.741
20.	Al McGuire	Belmont Abbey	1958-64		
		Marquette	1965-77	406-142	.741
21.	Jim Boeheim	Syracuse	1977-present	750-264	.740
22.	Lute Olson	Long Beach State	1974		
		Iowa	1975-83		
		Arizona	1984-present	761-269	.739
23.	Phog Allen	Baker	1906-1908		
		Haskell	1909		
		C. Missouri	1913-1919		
		Kansas	1908-09, 1920-56	746-264	.739
24.	Everett Case	North Carolina State	1947-64	377-134	.738
25.	Bob Huggins	Walsh	1981-83		
		Akron	1985-89		
		Cincinnati	1990-2005		
		Kansas State	2006	590-211	.737

Ray Mear's Players in Pro Basketball

Howard Bayne   Kentucky Colonels, ABA, 1967-68

Tom Boerwinkle   1st round pick Bulls 1968, Bulls 1968-78

Orb Bowling   Kentucky Colonels, ABA, 1967-68

Bobby Croft   Kentucky Colonels, ABA, Texas Chaparrals, ABA, 1970-71

Terry Crosby   Kansas City Kings, 1979-80

Ernie Grunfeld   1st round pick Bucks, 1977, Bucks, 1977-79, Kansas City King, 1979-82, New York Knicks, 1982-86

Bobby Hogsett   Detroit Pistons, 1966-67

Reggie Johnson   1st round pick San Antonio Spurs 1980, Spurs 1980-81, Cleveland Cavaliers 1981-82, Kansas City Kings 1982-83, Philadelphia 76ers 1983, New Jersey Nets 1983-84

Bernard King   1st round pick New Jersey Nets 1977, Nets 1977-79, Utah Jazz 1979-80, Golden State Warriors, 1981-82, New York Knicks 1982-87, Washington Bullets 1987-92, New Jersey Nets 1992-93

Len Kosmalski   1974-76, Kansas City Kings

Red Robbins   1967-70 New Orleans of ABA, 1970-72 Utah Stars of ABA, 1972-73 San Diego of ABA, 1973-74 Kentucky Colonels of ABA, 1974-75 Virginia Squires of ABA

Ron Widby   1967-68, New Orleans Bucs of ABA

Tennessee Lettermen and Assistants Under Mears

Lettermen

Doug Ashworth, 1974-76
Howard Bayne, 1964-66
David Bell, 1967
Bert Bertelkamp, 1977
Tom Boerwinkle, 1967-68
Bill Booth, 1963
Orb Bowling, 1963
Bob Brykalski, 1975
Don Campbell, 1970
Austin Clark, 1974-76
Wes Coffman, 1967-68
Jimmy Cornwall, 1965-66
Bobby Croft, 1968-70
Terry Crosby, 1976-77
Johnny Darden, 1976-77
A.W. Davis, 1963-65
Mike Disney, 1963
Mike Edwards, 1971-73
Sid Elliott, 1962-64
Jimmy England, 1969-71
Jim Finley, 1964
Ernie Grunfeld, 1974-77
Bobby Jack Guinn, 1967
Bill Hann, 1967-69
Greg Hawkins, 1971
Tom Hendrix, 1966-68
Steve Hirschhorn, 1972
Bobby Hogsett, 1963, 1964, 1966
Mike Jackson, 1975-77
Don Johnson, 1969-71

Reggie Johnson, 1977, 78-79-80
Dick Johnston, 1969-71
Tim Joyce, 1975
Bill Justus, 1967-69
Rudy Kinard, 1969-70
Bernard King, 1975-77
Len Kosmalski, 1972-74
Larry Mansfield, 1968
David Moss, 1974
Kerry Myers, 1968, 1970
Larry McIntosh, 1964-66
Jerry Parker, 1963
Roger Peltz, 1971
Mac Petty, 1967-68
Skip Plotnicki, 1965
Lloyd Richardson, 1971-72-73
Austin "Red" Robbins, 1965-66
Pat Robinette, 1963-65
Larry Robinson, 1972-73
Danny Schultz, 1963-64
Bill Seale, 1974
John Snow, 1972-74
Chuck Threeths, 1977, 79-80
Wayne Tomlinson, 1972-74
Eddie Voelker, 1971-73
Ron Widby, 1965-67
Tommy Wilson, 1963
Jim Woodall, 1969-71
Rodney Woods, 1973-75
Bill Young, 1967

Assistants

Bill Gibbs, 1962-64
Tommy Bartlett, 1962-66
Jerry Parker, 1964-66
Sid Elliott, 1964-65
Stu Aberdeen, 1966-77
Sid Hatfield, 1967-70

A.W. Davis, 1969-75
Marty Morris, 1971-74
Frank Comunale, 1974-76
Cliff Wettig, 1975-77
Tom Deaton, 1976-77
Frank Harrell, 1977

Season-By-Season Tennessee Records
1962-63 (13-11)
SEC Record (6-8, seventh)
Captain: Jerry Parker
Highest National Ranking: Unranked

Tennessee Score	Opponent	Opponent Score	Playing Site
61	East Tennessee State	52	Home
75	Rice	52	Home
63	Xavier	48	Home
65	Sewanee	45	Home
73	The Citadel	56	Home
47	Missouri	54	Columbia
51	Evansville	68	Evansville
Sun Bowl Classic			
57	Texas Western	77	El Paso
59	Denver	58	El Paso
66	Florida State	65	Home
50	Vanderbilt	68	Home
77	Tulane	70	New Orleans
60	LSU	61	Baton Rouge
78	Kentucky	69	Lexington
69	Georgia Tech	73	Atlanta
94	Georgia	65	Home
73	Florida	84	Home
59	Mississippi State	63	Starkville
78	Mississippi	85	Oxford
72	Vanderbilt	74	Home
60	Georgia Tech	72	Home
73	Alabama	60	Home
55	Auburn	47	Home
63	Kentucky	55	Home

Leading Scorers		Rebound Leader	
Danny Schultz, G	15.9	A.W. Davis, F	8.2
A.W. Davis, F	14.9		
Sid Elliott, F	10.1		
Jerry Parker, G	8.4		
Orb Bowling, C	8.2		

1963-64 Season
Overall Record: 16-8
SEC Record: 9-5 (second)
Captain: Sid Elliott
Highest National Ranking: Unranked

Tennessee Score	Opponent	Opponent Score	Playing Site
71	VMI	59	Home
57	Xavier	69	Cincinnati
56	Rice	61	Houston
48	East Tenn. State	47	Johnson City
55	Sewanee	31	Home
Virginia Tech Tournament			
70	Maryland	59	Blacksburg
81	Virginia Tech	60	Blacksburg
Gulf South Classic			
77	Arkansas	57	Shreveport
70	Centenary	63	Shreveport
68	Phillips 66 (Exh.)	55	Home
82	Tulane	55	Home
62	LSU	58	Home
57	Kentucky	66	Lexington
96	Ft. Knox (Exh.)	56	Home
62	Duke (2 OTs)	67	Durham
83	Georgia Tech	63	Home
67	Georgia	79	Athens
82	Mississippi State	58	Home
65	Vanderbilt	62	Nashville
45	Georgia Tech	47	Atlanta
64	Alabama	67	Tuscaloosa
68	Auburn	62	Auburn
38	Kentucky	42	Home
59	Florida	58	Gainesville

Leading Scorers
Danny Schultz, G   18.3
A.W. Davis, F   17.3
Howard Bayne, F   8.7
Larry McIntosh, G   7.3
Sid Elliott, C   6.5

Leading Rebounder
Sid Elliott   7.8

1964-1965
Overall Record: 20-5
SEC Record: 12-4 (Second)
Captain: A.W. Davis
Highest National Ranking: No. 8

Tennessee Score	Opponent	Opponent Score	Playing Site
97	Richmond	66	Home
66	Georgia Tech	52	Atlanta
71	Sewanee	42	Home
79	Buffalo	54	Home
65	Florida State	43	Memphis
Far West Classic			
70	Portland	59	Portland
70	Oregon	63	Portland
27	Oregon State	48	Portland
72	Vanderbilt	77	Nashville
80	Tulane	63	New Orleans
58	LSU	54	Baton Rouge
77	Kentucky	58	Home
76	Georgia	57	Athens
55	Georgia Tech	48	Home
83	Georgia	49	Home
75	Florida	43	Home
77	Mississippi State	57	Home
96	Mississippi	50	Oxford
79	Vanderbilt	66	Home
58	Alabama	63	Tuscaloosa
69	Auburn	38	Home
60	Kentucky	61	Lexington
56	Florida	58	Gainesville
83	LSU	60	Home
102	Tulane	62	Home

Leading Scorers
A.W. Davis, F	19.6
Ron Widby, F	14.5
Larry McIntosh, G	12.2
Red Robbins, C	10.1
Howard Bayne, C	7.0

Leading Rebounder
Ron Widby, F	8.3

1965-1966
Overall Record: 18-8
SEC Record: 10-6 (tie third)
Captains: Larry McIntosh/Howard Bayne
Highest National Ranking: Unranked

Tennessee Score	Opponent	Opponent Score	Playing Site
63	Michigan	71	Ann Arbor
65	Quantico Marines (Exh.)	56	Home
50	Vanderbilt	53	Home
Gulf Coast Classic			
71	Louisiana Tech	55	Shreveport
49	Centenary	43	Shreveport
Rainbow Classic			
57	St. Louis	59	Honolulu
88	Hawaii	41	Honolulu
84	Hawaii Marines (Exh.)	54	Honolulu
64	Tulane	46	Home
82	Furman	46	Home
102	Mississippi	55	Home
52	Vanderbilt	53	Nashville
74	Mississippi State (2 OTs)	75	Starkville
47	Auburn	51	Auburn
83	Georgia Tech	48	Home
121	Mexico	42	Home
65	N.C. State	54	Memphis
91	Alabama	56	Home
87	LSU	59	Home
76	Florida	47	Home
100	Georgia	71	Home
90	Tulane	70	New Orleans
74	LSU	64	Baton Rouge
83	Georgia	59	Athens
63	Florida	67	Gainesville
64	Kentucky	78	Lexington
58	Georgia Tech	47	Atlanta
69	Kentucky	62	Knoxville

Leading Scorers

Ron Widby, F	17.3
Red Robbins, C	17.1
Jim Cornwall, G	8.9
Larry McIntosh, G	8.8
Tom Hendrix, G	7.6

Leading Rebounder

Red Robbins	12.6

1966-67
Overall Record: 21-7
SEC Record: 15-3 (first)
Captain: Ron Widby
Highest National Ranking: No. 8

Tennessee Score	Opponent	Opponent Score	Playing Site
72	Michigan	54	Home
67	SW Louisiana	52	Home
Volunteer Classic			
73	Auburn	49	Home
52	Clemson	44	Home
Sugar Bowl Classic			
53	Bradley	60	New Orleans
61	Boston College	68	New Orleans
87	Furman	49	Home
77	Alabama	52	Home
59	Vanderbilt	65	Nashville
87	Georgia	70	Athens
66	Florida	53	Gainesville
56	Florida	42	Home
52	Kentucky (2 OTs)	50	Lexington
62	Mississippi	49	Home
67	Mississippi State	45	Home
59	Georgia Tech	48	Home
53	Mississippi	56	Oxford
76	LSU	59	Baton Rouge
68	Georgia	36	Home
76	Kentucky	57	Home
70	Vanderbilt	53	Home
54	Auburn	45	Auburn
52	Alabama	53	Tuscaloosa
65	N.C. State	62	Greensboro
87	LSU.	60	Home
78	Miss. St. (3 OTs)	76	Starkville
NCAA Tournament			
52	Dayton	53	Evanston, Ill.
44	Indiana	51	Evanston, Ill.

Leading Scorers
Ron Widby, F — 22.1
Tom Boerwinkle, C — 12.0
Billy Justus, G — 11.2
Tom Hendrix, F — 10.0
Billy Hann, G — 4.9

Leading Rebounder
Tom Boerwinkle — 10.2

1967-1968
Overall Record: 20-6
SEC Record: (13-5, second)
Captain: Tom Hendrix
Highest National Ranking: No. 4

Tennessee Score	Opponent	Opponent Score	Playing Site
93	Richmond	45	Home
Vol Classic			
66	Illinois	42	Home
56	Tulsa	48	Home
81	Wake Forest	63	Home
Los Angeles Classic			
59	Iowa	64	Los Angeles
78	Southern Cal	68	Los Angeles
85	Utah State	63	Los Angeles
82	Alabama	63	Tuscaloosa
64	Vanderbilt	62	Home
77	Georgia	72	Home
67	Florida	52	Home
46	Florida	59	Gainesville
87	Kentucky	59	Home
66	Mississippi	65	Oxford
65	Mississippi State	57	Starkville
88	Mississippi	46	Home
87	LSU	67	Baton Rouge
43	Georgia	61	Athens
59	Kentucky	60	Lexington
63	Vanderbilt	75	Nashville
71	Georgia Tech	69	Atlanta
52	Auburn	53	Home
75	Alabama	56	Home
74	LSU	71	Home
63	Mississippi State	51	Home
63	Auburn	54	Auburn

Leading Scorers
Billy Justus, G   18.0
Tom Boerwinkle, C   15.2
Tom Hendrix, C   10.6
Billy Hann, G   10.2
Bobby Croft, C   8.3

Leading Rebounder
Tom Boerwinkle   11.3

1968-1969
Overall Record: 21-7
SEC Record (13-5, second)
Captain: Billy Justus
Highest National Ranking: No. 17

Tennessee Score	Opponent	Opponent Score	Playing Site
87	Buffalo	62	Home
66	Iowa State	72	Home
Vol Classic			
55	Oklahoma	49	Home
54	Southern Illinois	41	Home
72	Georgia Tech	41	Home
52	Tampa	51	Tampa, Fla.
57	Mississippi State	58	Starkville
59	Mississippi	54	Oxford
82	Georgia	67	Home
64	Florida	63	Home
66	Kentucky	69	Home
70	Alabama	43	Tuscaloosa
81	LSU	68	Baton Rouge
64	Auburn	59	Home
65	Vanderbilt	61	Home
80	Mississippi State	50	Home
61	Mississippi	45	Home
57	Georgia	55	Athens
63	Florida	65	Gainesville
87	LSU	63	Home
60	Auburn	71	Auburn
70	Vanderbilt	69	Home
69	Kentucky	84	Lexington
National Invitational Tournament			
67	Rutgers	51	New York City
75	Ohio U	64	New York City
58	Temple	63	New York City
64	Army	52	New York City

Leading Scorers		**Leading Rebounder**	
Billy Justus, G	16.3	Bobby Croft, C	8.9
Bobby Croft, C	15.2		
Jimmy England, G	12.3	**Assist Leader**	
Don Johnson, F	11.5	Billy Hann, G	6.2
Billy Hann, G	6.6		

1969-1970
Overall Record: 16-9
SEC Record: 10-8 (Fifth)
Captain: Bobby Croft
Highest National Ranking: No. 6

Tennessee Score	Opponent	Opponent Score	Playing Site
55	South Carolina	54	Columbia
66	Centenary	62	Home
Vol Classic			
71	Montana State	62	Home
55	LaSalle	47	Home
All-College Challenge			
82	St. Francis	59	Oklahoma City
68	Niagra	69	Oklahoma City
72	Memphis State	51	Oklahoma City
58	Mississippi State	56	Home
57	Mississippi	59	Home
56	Georgia	61	Athens
56	Florida	57	Gainesville
52	Kentucky	68	Lexington
103	Alabama	67	Home
59	LSU	71	Baton Rouge
55	Auburn	61	Auburn
77	Vanderbilt	72	Nashville
72	Mississippi State	60	Starkville
72	Oxford	60	Oxford
57	Georgia	55	Home
72	Florida	61	Home
77	Alabama	70	Tuscaloosa
88	LSU	87	Home
64	Auburn	77	Home
83	Vanderbilt	76	Home
69	Kentucky	86	Lexington

Leading Scorers		**Leading Rebounder**	
Jimmy England, G	19.4	Bobby Croft, C	9.6
Bobby Croft, C	17.2		
Don Johnson, F	14.0	**Assist Leader**	
Rudy Kinard, G	8.1	Jimmy England, G	2.5
Kerry Myers, G	4.6		

1970-71
Overall Record: 21-7
SEC Record: 13-5 (second)
Captain: Jimmy England
Highest National Ranking: No. 8

Tennessee Score	Opponent	Opponent Score	Playing Site
90	Northern Michigan	68	Home
79	Houston	58	Home
60	Wake Forest	59	Winston-Salem
Vol Classic			
79	San Francisco	59	Home
77	Providence	58	Home
89	Oregon State	61	Home
Trojan Classic			
65	Houston	68	Los Angeles
81	Michigan State	70	Los Angeles
67	Mississippi State	69	Starkville
98	Mississippi	85	Oxford
51	Georgia	47	Home
85	Florida	75	Home
75	Kentucky	71	Home
79	Alabama	62	Tuscaloosa
70	LSU	80	Baton Rouge
90	Auburn	68	Home
80	Vanderbilt	65	Home
88	Mississippi State	74	Home
80	Mississippi	74	Home
64	Georgia	61	Athens
55	Florida	56	Gainesville
89	Alabama	77	Home
88	LSU	67	Home
76	Auburn	71	Auburn
79	Vanderbilt	69	Nashville
78	Kentucky	84	Lexington
National Invitational Tournament			
84	St. John's	83	New York City
64	Duke	78	New York City

Leading Scorers
Jimmy England, G   20.6
Don Johnson, F   18.7
Mike Edwards, G   17.0
Jim Woodall, C   6.8
Lloyd Richardson, F 5.4

Leading Rebounder
Don Johnson, F   10.4

Assist Leader
Jimmy England, G   5.2*
*Denotes SEC Overall Leader for Season.

1971-1972
Overall Record: 19-6
SEC Record: 14-4 (tie first)
Captain: Lloyd Richardson
Highest National Ranking: No. 19

Tennessee Score	Opponent	Opponent Score	Playing Site
89	Cal Irvine	53	Home
65	Houston	67	Houston
	Vol Classic		
57	Penn State	55	Home
85	Michigan State	61	Home
	Quaker City Classic		
76	Manhattan	70	Philadelphia
67	Villanova	76	Philadelphia
61	Boston College	60	Philadelphia
84	Poland Olympic(Exh.)	74	Home
82	Mississippi State	49	Home
73	Mississippi	70	Home
59	Georgia	57	Athens
61	Florida	50	Gainesville
70	Kentucky	72	Lexington
79	Alabama	77	Home
62	LSU	63	Home
76	Auburn	67	Auburn
81	Vanderbilt	75	Nashville
71	Mississippi State	51	Starkville
68	Mississippi	58	Oxford
71	Georgia	68	Home
55	Florida	52	Home
67	Alabama	72	Tuscaloosa
78	LSU	66	Baton Rouge
80	Auburn	70	Home
87	Vanderbilt	74	Home
66	Kentucky	67	Home

Leading Scorers
Len Kosmalski, C   19.5
Mike Edwards, G   19.4
Larry Robinson, F   10.2
John Snow, G   10.1
Lloyd Richardson, F   7.1

Leading Rebounder
Larry Robinson, F   9.0

Assist Leader
Steve Hirschorn   3.6

1972-1973
Overall Record: 15-9
SEC Record: 13-5 (second)
Captain: Larry Robinson
Highest National Ranking: No. 14

Tennessee Score	Opponent	Opponent Score	Playing Site
55	South Carolina	45	Home
30	Marquette	56	Milwaukee
	Vol Classic		
87	Syracuse	83	Home
57	Missouri	67	Home
	ECAC Classic		
55	St. John's	56	New York City
62	Niagara	66	New York City
86	Mississippi State	67	Starkville
52	Mississippi	60	Oxford
79	Georgia	64	Home
75	Florida	56	Home
65	Kentucky	64	Home
56	Alabama	72	Tuscaloosa
73	LSU	71	Baton Rouge
82	Auburn	74	Home
72	Vanderbilt	62	Home
93	Mississippi State	76	Home
51	Mississippi	49	Home
85	Georgia	71	Athens
87	Florida	83	Gainesville
72	Alabama	71	Home
74	LSU	78	Home
74	Vanderbilt	86	Nashville
80	Auburn	72	Auburn
81	Kentucky	86	Lexington

Leading Scorers
Len Kosmalski, C   17.0
Mike Edwards, G   15.9
John Snow, G   13.1
Larry Robinson, F   11.7
Rodney Woods, G   9.8

Leading Rebounder
Larry Robinson, F   8.5

Assist Leader
Rodney Woods, G   5.9*

1973-1974
Overall Record: 17-9
SEC Record: 12-6 (second)
Captain: Len Kosmalski
Highest National Ranking: Unranked

Tennessee Score	Opponent	Opponent Score	Playing Site
80	North Texas State	71	Home
65	Marquette	67	Home
117	South Florida	90	Home
Vol Classic			
86	DePaul	61	Home
11	Temple	6	Home
Rainbow Classic			
79	Sub Pac (Exh.)	81	Honolulu
60	Providence	64	Honolulu
80	Santa Clara	76	Honolulu
89	Auburn	77	Auburn
73	Alabama	79	Alabama
57	Mississippi	69	Oxford
67	Kentucky	54	Home
75	Florida	72	Gainesville
65	Vanderbilt	82	Home
70	Mississippi State	61	Home
57	LSU	52	Baton Rouge
84	Georgia	70	Home
88	Auburn	80	Home
54	Alabama	73	Tuscaloosa
65	Mississippi	57	Home
58	Kentucky	61	Lexington
85	Florida	57	Home
59	Vanderbilt	53	Nashville
58	Mississippi State	62	Starkville
100	LSU	80	Home
97	Georgia	89	Athens
Conference Commissioners Tournament			
71	Indiana	73	St. Louis

Leading Scorers
Ernie Grunfeld, F   17.4
John Snow, G   16.4
Len Kosmalski, C   16.3
Rodney Woods, G   9.8
Wayne Tomlinson, F   4.6

Leading Rebounder
Len Kosmalski, C   9.8

Assist Leader
Rodney Woods, G   6.0*
*Denotes SEC Overall Leader for Season.

1974-1975
Overall Record: 18-8
SEC Record: 12-6 (tie third)
Captain: Rodney Woods
Highest National Ranking: No. 15

Tennessee Score	Opponent	Opponent Score	Playing Site
85	Wisconsin-Milwaukee	65	Home
100	St. Kilda (Exh.)	69	Home
74	Michigan	78	Ann Arbor

Vol Classic

86	Navy	59	Home
84	Harvard	59	Home

Big Sun Invitational

108	Columbia	73	St. Petersburg, Fla.
99	Missouri	77	St. Petersburg, Fla.
115	Vermont	66	Home
96	Auburn	81	Home
78	Alabama	82	Tuscaloosa
102	Mississippi	82	Home
82	Kentucky	88	Lexington
59	Florida	56	Home
65	Vanderbilt	61	Nashville
97	Mississippi State	87	Starkville
99	LSU	79	Home
105	Georgia	69	Athens
59	Auburn	62	Auburn
65	Alabama	71	Home
81	Mississippi	88	Oxford
103	Kentucky	98	Home
85	Florida	84	Gainesville
75	Vanderbilt	71	Home
109	Mississippi State	83	Home
87	LSU	94	Baton Rouge
95	Georgia	74	Home

NCIT Tournament

58	Bowling Green	67	Louisville

Leading Scorers
Bernard King, F — 26.4
*Ernie Grunfeld, F — 23.8
Mike Jackson, G — 13.3
Rodney Woods, G — 8.7
Doug Ashworth, C — 8.4

Leading Rebounder
Bernard King, F — 12.5

Assist Leader
Rodney Woods, G — 8.7*
*Denotes SEC Overall Leader for Season.

1975-1976
Overall Record: 21-6
SEC Record: 14-4 (second)
Captain: Doug Ashworth
Highest National Ranking: No. 7

Tennessee Score	Opponent	Opponent Score	Playing Site
81	Biscayne	63	Home
86	Duke	80	Durham
82	Michigan	81	Home
70	St. John's	79	New York City
119	St. Mary's Canada (Exh.).	70	Home
Vol Classic			
99	Army	79	Home
77	Clemson	66	Home
Sugar Bowl Classic			
77	Pennsylvania	70	New Orleans
97	Tulane	73	New Orleans
79	Georgia	73	Athens
90	Kentucky (OT)	88	Lexington
66	Vanderbilt	77	Nashville
93	Florida	84	Home
83	Auburn	78	Home
56	Mississippi	53	Oxford
105	LSU	92	Baton Rouge
80	Alabama	74	Home
75	Mississippi State	66	Home
92	Kentucky	85	Home
73	Vanderbilt	59	Home
69	Florida	72	Gainesville
72	Auburn (OT)	73	Auburn
105	Mississippi	81	Home
80	LSU	71	Home
90	Alabama (2 OTs)	93	Tuscaloosa
78	Mississippi State	76	Starkville
86	Georgia	70	Home
NCAA Tournament			
75	VMI	81	Charlotte

Leading Scorers		**Leading Rebounder**	
Ernie Grunfeld, F	25.3*	Bernard King, F	13.0*
Bernard King, F	25.2	**Assist Leader**	
Mike Jackson, G	16.7	Johnny Darden, G	6.1
Doug Ashworth, C	5.7		
Johnny Darden, G	5.1	*Denotes SEC Overall Leader for Season.	

1976-1977
Overall Record: 22-6
SEC Record: 16-2 (tie first)
Captains: Mike Jackson and Ernie Grunfeld
Highest National Ranking: No. 7

Tennessee Score	Opponent	Opponent Score	Playing Site
98	St. Kilda (Exh.)	72	Home
94	South Florida	74	Home
69	UNC-Charlotte	67	Home
78	Duke	81	Home
Utah Classic			
77	San Francisco	86	Salt Lake City
99	Seton Hall	90	Salt Lake City
Vol Classic			
92	LaSalle	85	Home
86	St. John's	81	Home
97	Xavier	73	Home
Real Madrid Christmas Tournament			
98	Nice, France (Exh.)	95	Madrid, Spain
112	African All-Stars (Exh.)	85	Madrid, Spain
103	Read Madrid (Exh.)	113	Madrid, Spain
73	Vanderbilt	69	Nashville
87	Auburn	79	Auburn
92	Florida	82	Home
71	Kentucky	67	Lexington
108	LSU	102	Baton Rouge
86	Mississippi	72	Oxford
102	Alabama	93	Home
68	Mississippi State	59	Home
89	UCLA	103	Atlanta
106	Georgia	82	Home
93	Auburn	83	Auburn
76	Florida	80	Gainesville
91	LSU	64	Home
87	Mississippi	75	Home
92	Alabama	89	Tuscaloosa
76	Mississippi State	68	Starkville
76	Georgia	83	Athens
81	Kentucky	79	Home
65	Vanderbilt	55	Home
NCAA Tournament			
88	Syracuse (OT)	93	Baton Rouge

Leading Scorers
Bernard King, F   25.8*
Ernie Grunfeld, F   22.8
Mike Jackson, G   15.4
Reggie Johnson, C   11.0
Johnny Darden, G   5.6

Leading Rebounder
Bernard King, F   14.3*

Assist Leader
Johnny Darden, G   8.2
*Denotes SEC Overall Leader for Season.

All-Americans At Tennessee Under Ray Mears

1964—Danny Schultz, Converse
1965—A.W. Davis, Helms, Basketball Writers
1966—Red Robbins, Helms
1967—Ron Widby, Helms, Associated Press
1968—Tom Boerwinkle, Helms
1969—Billy Justus, Helms
1971—Jimmy England, Helms
1975—Bernard King, Helms
1976—Bernard King, Helms, Basketball Writers
1976—Ernie Grunfeld, Helms
1977—Bernard King, Helms, UPI, AP, Basketball Writers, Converse, NCAA
1977—Ernie Grunfeld, Basketball Writers, Converse, Helms

All-SEC First Team Players Under Ray Mears

1963—Danny Schultz
1964—Danny Schultz, A.W. Davis
1965—A.W. Davis
1966—Red Robbins, Ron Widby
1967—[x]Ron Widby, Tom Boerwinkle
1968—Tom Boerwinkle, Billy Justus
1969—Billy Justus
1970—Bobby Croft, Jimmy England
1971—Jimmy England, Don Johnson
1972— [x]Mike Edwards, Len Kosmalski
1973—Mike Edwards, Len Kosmalski
1974—Len Kosmalski, Ernie Grunfeld
1975—Ernie Grunfeld, [x]Bernard King
1976—[x]Bernard King, [x]Ernie Grunfeld
1977—[x]Bernard King, [x]Ernie Grunfeld

[x]SEC Player of the Year.

About The Author

Ron Bliss is a 1969 University of Iowa journalism graduate who attended graduate school before beginning active duty in the U.S. Army as an officer in 1969. He served as an assistant in the sports information department at Iowa before leaving for the Army and eventual service in the Vietnam War where he earned a Bronze Star Medal. He was released from the Army in 1973 and moved to Kingsport, Tennessee. He covered the University of Tennessee basketball program when Ernie Grunfeld was a freshman in 1973-74. He is one of the very few writers still covering Tennessee basketball who covered the Vols during the glory days of the Mid-1970s when Ray Mears enjoyed some of his greatest success in Knoxville.

Bliss was promoted to executive sports editor of the *Kingsport Times-News* in 1975 and remained in that position until leaving for a 16-month period in 1983 and 1984 for a job in Alabama. He returned to the *Times-News* in 1984 and remained there until resigning in the summer of 2004 to start an on-line sports page, *TriCitiesSports.com*. It later expanded to include a twice-monthly sports newspaper. He's been honored on the elite registry of *Oxford's Who's Who of Extraordinary Professionals* as well as the *Cambridge Who's Who of Professionals* and was several times voted one of the top columnists in the Tri-Cities, Northeast Tennessee/Southwest Virginia area. Twice his *Times-News* sports sections were ranked as high as second in Tennessee. He served as president of the Tennessee Sports Writers Association in 1997 and 1998 and also served as an officer in the group in some capacity for 10 years. He has been a Heisman Trophy voter since 1981.

Bliss is married to the former Rachael Roberts, who he met in the Journalism Department at Iowa in 1967. They are parents of five children—including two Tennessee graduates (Robert and Josh) and a California-Berkeley graduate [Randee (Miranda)]. Robert went on to earn a M.S. degree from Stanford, Randee an M.A. from Harvard, and Josh an M.A. from Brown University and a Law Degree from New York University. Robert now lives in Alviso, California, Randee in Asheville, North Carolina, and Josh in New York City. Renee attended Tennessee for two years and is now living in Portland, Oregon, and working as a barista, while Ryan is a sophomore at Tennessee in Knoxville this fall.

Bliss had known Coach Mears since those early days of his career in Kingsport and renewed the acquaintance after Mears retired as athletic director at Tennessee-Martin and moved to Loudon County near Knoxville. Mears started coming to Kingsport on a somewhat regular basis to visit two of his sons, Steve and Matt, who both lived there at the time. Steve has since relocated to Greeneville. Mears asked Bliss to write this book.

Bliss' aim in writing this book is to preserve the history of the era and the many colorful stories that came from it, including how use of the orange colors by Tennessee fans came about. *Its main purpose is to honor Mears as the sports legend he is.*